Théâtre de la Mode

THEATER OF FASHION

Théâtre de la Mode

Fashion Dolls:
The Survival of Haute Couture

Essays by
Edmonde Charles-Roux
Herbert R. Lottman
Stanley Garfinkel
Nadine Gasc
Colleen Schafroth and Betty Long-Schleif

Essay and Fashion Photographs
by David Seidner

Original Edition Edited by
Susan Train
with
Eugène Clarence Braun-Munk

Palmer/Pletsch Publishing

At left: drawing by Eliane Bonabel illustrating a special catalogue
made for Robert Ricci (Théâtre de la Mode, Paris, March 1945).

The original revival of this collection was due to the efforts of many, many people living and working around the world. Sadly, since the publication of the first catalog in 1990 Eliane Bonabel, Stanley Garfinkel, Madame Grès, Robert Ricci, Stephen de Petri, Boris Kochno, Jean-Denis Malclès, and David Seidner have passed on. This edition is dedicated to their memories.

Second Revised Edition © 2002 Maryhill Museum of Art
Published by Palmer/Pletsch Inc.
1801 NW Upshur, Portland, Oregon 97209
1-800-728-3784
www.palmerpletsch.com

Library of Congress Control Number: 2002109517
Printed in the USA

First Edition © 1990 Editions du May, 116, rue du Bac, 75007 Paris
Edipress-Livres SA, Lausanne
First published in the United States of America in 1991
by Rizzoli International Publications, Inc., New York

ISBN 0-935278-56-7

Contents

Message from the Publisher:

When I lived in Hood River, Oregon, during the 1950s and early '60s, my mother took me to a fairly new museum in southern Washington, Maryhill Museum of Art. There, I marveled at the coronation gown of Queen Marie of Roumania and a few of those mysterious 27" wire dolls scattered around in glass boxes – "tay-ah-tra de la mode." I could only imagine what their history entailed. As a preteen, I found the museum very interesting and eclectic, like one's own home. I still have the postcards I bought from those memorable visits, not realizing that as an adult our paths would cross again.

We moved to Montana, but I came back to Oregon to study fashion design at Oregon State University. In the 1970s I authored several sewing books and went on to become a publisher of sewing, image, and home decorating books, headquartered in Portland, Oregon. I also began to design for Vogue then McCall's pattern companies. After traveling the world teaching for fifteen years, I started Sewing Vacation Workshops in Portland. In the mid-1990s, I began taking our couture workshop students to Maryhill for a behind-the-scenes closeup viewing of the dolls of Théâtre de la Mode. Collections Manager Betty Long-Schleif held our students in awe as she discussed the details on the clothing she showed.

In 1990, couture sewing expert Roberta Carr traveled with the Board of Trustees of Maryhill to Paris for the grand reopening of Théâtre de la Mode. When we published her book, Couture, the Art of Fine Sewing, *in 1993, she asked if it could include the story of that event.*

Over many years of trips to Maryhill with my couture workshop, I kept hearing that everyone wished the catalogue from the 1991 exhibition at the Metropolitan Museum of Art was still in print. As a publisher with a passion for the museum and especially the Théâtre collection, two years ago I suggested Palmer/Pletsch might be interested. After a year of trying to get the film, photo rights, and publishing rights, we tabled the idea due to what was looking like unsurmountable obstacles.

Then, knowing anything can be done if you want it badly enough (I am no different from the creators of those dolls), I found that by reformatting the book and collecting some of the original photos, we could do it. In addition, there is the destiny factor. UFDC (United Federation of Doll Collectors) decided to adopt the new book for its 2002 convention because of the Tonner Doll Company connection with Maryhill. This was the final boost we needed. When we realized that the second edition could be an enhancement of the first, we added photos of the sets re-created for the 1990 reopening in Paris. We have also enlarged the photos in the catalogue beginning on page 129 so that the clothing details can be seen better...a plus for students of fashion and designers as well as sewers. Since the rediscovery of the dolls, a lot has happened, so we asked Betty Long-Schleif and Maryhill Director Colleen Schafroth to add an Epilogue – the story of the mannequins since 1990. They tell the story of their restoration, their jewelry, their travels around the world, and the licensing of the Tonner limited edition dolls.

Théâtre de la Mode is MY passion, but in some magical way, it becomes the passion of nearly everyone who has ever seen it or been involved with it. Its story evokes empathy for those who endured the war, admiration for the artists who came together to show the world that their industry and hope couldn't be obliterated by shortages and devastation, and emotion for even a preteen in the '50s who keeps reconnecting with the magic.

Pati Palmer, President
Palmer/Pletsch Publishing

Foreword to the First Edition

For nearly four decades visitors to Maryhill Museum of Art have been enchanted by the mannequins of the Théâtre de la Mode. It is no wonder that visitors to the exhibition, first at the Musée des Arts de la Mode in Paris, then at the Costume Institute of the Metropolitan Museum of Art, are intrigued and delighted to see the mannequins restored to their original state and "choreographed" before replicas of nine of the original twelve theatrical sets. The creation of the Théâtre de la Mode was a remarkable feat, a phenomenon of post-World War II Paris forged by the spirit of the times. The essays in this book fully address the uniqueness of the original Théâtre de la Mode project.

In 1946, the last venue for the Théâtre de la Mode was the M.H. de Young Memorial Museum in San Francisco. At the close of the exhibition the figurines were stored at the City of Paris department store (now Neiman Marcus) pending a decision on future exhibitions or their return to Paris. Finally, Paul Verdier, owner of the City of Paris and president of the Board of Trustees for the California Legion of Honor, wrote to the Chambre Syndicale de la Couture suggesting that the dolls be preserved at the Maryhill Museum of Art. It was Alma de Bretteville Spreckels, a major benefactor of both Maryhill and the Legion of Honor, who had proposed this solution, which was approved at an executive meeting of the Chambre Syndicale in September 1951. The mannequins arrived at Maryhill Museum in 1952 and since then have been the most appealing exhibit of the French decorative arts collection. It was with both sadness and anticipation that we sent them to Paris in 1988 for restoration and exhibition.

By regarding the mannequins of the Théâtre de la Mode as *objets d'art*, creations born of collective innovation, Mr. Verdier and Mrs. Spreckels assured the survival of this historically significant collection. Through their acts of inspired foresight, these individuals unknowingly addressed a critical responsibility of today's museum: to serve as an arbiter in the challenge to preserve objects that best elucidate the past. Thus, icons of popular culture ultimately become museum artifacts for the enjoyment and edification of future generations. The joint efforts of the Musée des Arts de la Mode, the Costume Institute, and Maryhill Museum of Art to restore the mannequins to their former grandeur fulfill the vision of Mr. Verdier, Mrs. Spreckels, the Chambre Syndicale, and others.

The organizers of this exhibition have enjoyed a spirit of collaboration not unlike that of the original artists of the Théâtre de la Mode. The Maryhill Board of Trustees and I extend special gratitude to Susan Train, Paris Bureau Chief of Condé Nast Publications Inc. and editor of this book, and Stanley Garfinkel, professor of history at Kent State University, for their original idea and persistent efforts to restore and exhibit the mannequins once again in Paris. We gratefully acknowledge Pierre Provoyeur, curator in chief of the Musée des Arts de la Mode; Nadine Gasc, curator, head of the fashion and textiles department of the Musée des Arts de la Mode; and Katell le Bourhis, associate curator for special projects of the Costume Institute of the Metropolitan Museum of Art, for their leadership and scholarship in bringing the revitalized Théâtre de la Mode before French and American audiences. Maryhill is particularly pleased that thanks to Anne Surgers, nine sets have been brilliantly recreated so that the Théâtre de la Mode can be permanently shown as a whole. The advice and support of Eliane Bonabel, André Beaurepaire, and Jean-Denis Malclès have been invaluable. It is with special fondness that we remember the late Stephen de Pietri who provided the artistic direction for the exhibition. Generous financial support from the Union Centrale des Arts Décoratifs, the Metropolitan Museum of Art, the Chambre Syndicale de la Couture, and The Fashion Foundation (Tokyo) have made the exhibition and this handsome book possible. We also thank Pierre de Rohan Chabot of TransAtlantic Video in Paris and Tom Ball of Telos Video in Cleveland, Ohio, for their contributions to this project.

Kenneth Clark defined a masterpiece as "the work of an artist of genius who has been absorbed by the spirit of the time in a way that has made his individual experiences universal." If this is true, then the Théâtre de la Mode is truly a collective masterpiece that visually summarizes the *esprit de corps* and *esprit du temps* of 1945–46 in clothes, accessories, and theatrical sets. Maryhill Museum of Art and our visitors are the ultimate and long-term beneficiaries of this exhibition project. We look forward to the return of the Théâtre de la Mode and to our role as custodians of these international "ambassadors of fashion."

Linda Brady Tesner,
Director, Maryhill Museum of Art,
1982-1991

Here, and on the cover – the opera boxes and the stage of the décor by Christian Bérard. Painter, fashion illustrator, and one of the most brilliant and well-known set designers for both opera and theater at that time, Bérard, as artistic director, made of the whole exhibition a tribute to illusion and imagination.

Foreword to the Second Edition

Since its spectacular revival in 1990, the Théâtre de la Mode has continued to delight audiences around the world. It has been exhibited in whole or in part in Paris, London, Tokyo, New York, Honolulu, Baltimore, and Portland, Oregon. Its fame has become far-reaching, attracting the attention of fashion experts as well as doll enthusiasts around the globe. Its influence has been astounding. It has inspired fashion and stage designers, artists and artisans, a wide range of merchandise from magnets to scarves, and more recently the development of limited-edition dolls by the Robert Tonner Doll Company. Created in the Twentieth century, the Théâtre de la Mode will breathe new life into the word haute couture. The result of this attention, the need to know about the Théâtre de la Mode, has brought about a new edition of the original exhibition catalogue.

Any project of this magnitude can be accomplished only with the dedicated help and hard work of many. But someone needs to start the ball rolling. In this case, it was Donna and Oliver Hidden. Since they first saw Théâtre de la Mode years ago, their passion for the it has remained strong. They not only enthusiastically supported the publication of this new edition, but underwrote the initial costs. Without them I can only say that this book would never have been published.

Others, too, have played a vital role in the publication of this book. I gratefully acknowledge the help and support of Susan Train. Her love and devotion to the Théâtre de la Mode has no bounds. Since her personal rediscovery of the dolls over a decade ago, she has worked tirelessly on their behalf. Indeed, without her willingness and dedication this edition may have never made it to press.

Finally, although not least, I must also sincerely, and appreciatively, thank two staffers at Maryhill Museum of Art, Betty Long-Schleif and Patricia Perry. Because of their passion for the Théâtre de la Mode, they have stubbornly persevered in the publication of this book. Without their hard work, the Théâtre de la Mode might have slipped back into history again.

Colleen Schafroth
Executive Director, Maryhill Museum of Art

Introduction

Susan Train

Susan Train was Paris fashion editor for American Vogue *from 1951 to 1985 when she became Condé Nast Publications Paris Bureau Chief. In 1990 she was made a Chevalier de l'Ordres des Arts et des Lettres for her contribution to the world of fashion and notably for her extensive research and dedication to the Théâtre de la Mode exhibition at the Musée des Arts de la Mode, Paris, for which she was guest curator. So that the fabulous story of the dolls should never again be lost, she set her heart on this book, and on its republication.*

They have a magical aura about them, these little dolls of the Théâtre de la Mode. Everyone who has approached them in the years we have been working on their return to France, the exhibition, and this book, has fallen under their spell. Many people believe that inanimate objects somehow become imbued with a life of their own – perhaps breathed into them by their creators – and it is not difficult to imagine that these little *chefs-d'œuvre* come to life, as in the fairy tales of our childhood, when the lights go out and they are alone. Perhaps it is because they represent so many things that they elicit such a strangely emotional reaction. Born at a moment in history and under circumstances that were more than difficult, but in an *élan* of solidarity and hope for the future, they stand also for the creative ability, skills, and pride in perfection of detail of the artisans, couturiers, and artists of France. Their message is as strong today as it was in 1945-1946 when they carried it through Europe and to the United States and, inanimate though they appear to be, they are in fact, like the phoenix, a symbol of life.

I first heard about the Théâtre de la Mode in the 1950s from Michel de Brunhoff, editor-in-chief of French *Vogue*. Very young and very green, I had been parachuted into his *rédaction* by the head office of Vogue in America to be their correspondent in Paris. My qualifications were small: a recommendation by my adored Bettina Ballard, the fashion director, an ability to get by in the language; and an irrevocable passion for Paris and all things French. Michel was to take my fashion education in hand. I was enthralled by his stories of days gone by; and the little dolls of the Théâtre de la Mode, dressed by the couturiers and placed in sets designed by well-known artists, aroused my imagination to a frenzy. But all my efforts to discover their whereabouts or even to see photographs were met with Gallic shrugs...total amnesia seemed to have set in, "fashion is so ephemeral," and I was finally forced to admit defeat.

In 1985, when Professor Garfinkel told me he had discovered the dolls at the Maryhill Museum in Goldendale, Washington, my old obsession was reborn. I was greatly encouraged by Pierre Bergé, the president of Yves Saint-Laurent, the first person to whom I told the story. He promised his help (and amply fulfilled his promise) for my plan to bring the dolls back to Paris and exhibit them in the new fashion museum, then in construction, by a quirk of fate in the Pavillon Marsan where they had originated. With Pierre's backing I felt assured of success. And so I went to Maryhill.

One hundred miles from Portland, Oregon, up the gorge of the Columbia River, in spectacular countryside and splendid isolation on a bluff overlooking the river, stands the Maryhill Museum – the folly of an eccentric American, Sam Hill, friend of Loïe Fuller and Queen Marie of Roumania.

It was February and there was snow on the ground and icicles hanging from the roof. The museum was closed to the public, except for the one room in which then-director Linda Brady Tesner and her small staff were working. But the dolls! Some were on display in vitrines, some in boxes in the storage room; all had such presence and evoked Paris so strongly that I was transported as if by a time capsule back to my earliest days as a student and the first fashion collection I ever saw. My determination to bring them home to Paris, if only for a visit, redoubled.

And here is the result, and here I must thank all my friends in France, England, and the United States who have not only listened at length and shared my enthusiasm for this project (and they know who they are!) but also to those without whom it would never have come to be. First of all to my editorial director, Alexander Liberman, without whose approval and permission I would not have had the time to spend; to Diana Vreeland whose encouragement was very precious to me; and special thanks to Diana Edkins, curator and permissions editor of Condé Nast Publications Inc., for her invaluable advice and assistance. To Jacques Mouclier, president of the French Couture Federation, who uncovered a treasure of forgotten archives under the eaves, who gave me carte blanche to do my research, and who has supported the project both morally and financially through many a trial and tribulation. He is the hero of this story. To Stephen de Pietri who went straight to work and gave so much of his valuable time long before the exhibition had become a reality. To Eliane Bonabel who lived every stage of the original Théâtre de la Mode in Paris and on its travels, whose memory has been invaluable, and who has helped to restore "her" dolls to their original state. To Patricia del Pra and the staff of the Restoration of Versailles responsible for restoring the clothes and the heads. To Alexandre de Paris and his aide, Hinda Antereux, who worked miracles for the coiffures – imagine not having been to the hairdresser in forty-four years! To Massaro who ensured that a number of the dolls would not have to go barefooted. To David Seidner who struggled and suffered with these inanimate creatures to bring them back to life on film. To Yvonne Brunhammer, curator in chief of the Musée des Arts décoratifs, who always gave us her support. And most specially to Nadine Gasc, whose passion for the dolls is as great as mine. Without her expertise, her professionalism, and her hard labor neither the exhibition nor this book would have had the necessary scientific rigor.

My thanks also to Jean-François Gonthier of Edipress and Jacques Péron of Editions du May for believing in this book and to Eugene Braun-Munk for bringing them into the orbit of the Théâtre de la Mode. To the authors, Edmonde Charles-Roux, Herbert Lottman, Stanley Garfinkel, and Nadine Gasc, who were intrigued by the subject and accepted to write about it. To Lesley Blanch for her translation and her editorial counsel, to Jacqueline Horscher of Vogue Pattern Service, who brought her expertise to the Catalogue Raisonné, and to Nina de Voogd for working against short deadlines. To all the teams for both the exhibition and the book who helped so much to bring them about – in particular Denise Dubois and Sylvie Zawadski at the Chambre Syndicale; Véronique Belloir, assistant to Nadine Gasc; and Richard Medioni, Marlyne Kherlakian and Dominique Faber of the Editions du May.

I would like to dedicate this book with great affection to Robert Ricci whose idea the Théâtre de la Mode was at its origin. I am happy to think he knew of its rebirth – I wish he were here to see it.

Cover drawing by Christian Bérard for the catalogue of the exhibition (Théâtre de la Mode, Paris, March 1945).

The Théâtre de la Mode or the Return of Hope

Edmonde Charles-Roux of the Académie Goncourt

When the news reached us it was considered highly inconvenient. A war correspondent announced her arrival. She was one of the London War Correspondents Corps and was to make a reportage on the Alsatian front. It was fiendishly cold in February 1945. The German breakthrough in the Bitche region had flung all our reserve units around Strasbourg. The offensive launched by the Reich had been halted at the eleventh hour, but a large number of Germans were still lurking in the region and the division to which I was posted in the capacity of welfare assistant was in no mood for visitors. Colmar had only just been liberated. There were ruins everywhere; ruins and the dead. What were we to do with this war correspondent? She was to be in my charge, and at headquarters they specified that she was called Lee Miller and that the name meant nothing to them. Lee Miller! So it was she! That name, pronounced there in Alsace, in such circumstances, had the worst possible effect on me. It was not the place or the time for old memories and bygone images of ourselves now that past and present were still locked in mortal combat. This person, this Lee Miller whom I did not even know, was nevertheless the symbol of all that war had rendered unreal, almost unimaginable, a vanished world of high Parisian society with its brilliance, its salons, and its luxury, the Paris of my adolescence, of my first balls, a prewar world. All I knew of Lee Miller was what I had heard during those interminable icy evenings of the Occupation. Painters and writers who had taken refuge in Marseilles, with whom I was linked, had often spoken of her. It was at the home of Countess Pastré. Boris Kochno, Christian Bérard, Hans Namuth, and Jean Cocteau had all known Lee during her early days in Paris. She had posed for legendary photographers such as Hoyningen-Huene and Man Ray, whose assistant and great love she had been. She had become a photographer herself before appearing as a living statue in Cocteau's first film, *Blood of a Poet*.

And now this living statue was here among us, in flesh and blood. I had always heard of her beauty, and Lee did not belie her reputation. She indeed seemed extraordinarily beautiful, against a background of

March 1945: The curtain of the Théâtre de la Mode rises on a Paris scarred by four years of Occupation. But the dream-like décor created by Jean Cocteau is also symbolic of hope reborn and peace soon to come...fashion and luxury representing a lost paradise and a part of prestige to be reconquered.

ruins, in her strict khaki uniform. Here was a woman who symbolized this particular moment in time. There was an air of English chic about her, something which the Women's Forces of Britain exemplified – the Old World of Europe at war, possessing the secret of discretion and the sober elegance of well-cut uniforms worn well. They alone, I thought, possessed the discipline of good grooming. We French women were otherwise – were, in short, the very antithesis. Did we lack discipline? That would be an oversimplification. At that time we wore anything we could lay our hands on, come-by-chance bits and pieces. My skirt was contrived from a baggy pair of G.I. pants, my down-at-heel shoes were of uncertain origin. Nothing of my turnout seemed fit for the occasion, which added to my embarrassment. However well or badly dressed, I must receive this war correspondent sent by *Vogue*, whose mission was to photograph the harsh snowbound Alsatian scene: there, where the wounded were lodged in churches, the French Women's Auxiliary Forces were working at innumerable tasks, and the Foreign Legion was marching rapidly toward the Rhine. The Rhine...the Rhine...we thought of little else. Nevertheless, the living statue, a legend in the Paris of the '30s, who frequented eclectic salons such as that of the Viscountess de Noailles, who glittered in the champagne world of princes and maharajas, whose charms enflamed so many hearts and roused the jealousy of so many celebrated artists, impressed me profoundly.

It was during an expedition by jeep through streets of gutted houses and after a visit to a church whose belfry stood bell-less where Lee had photographed a nun whose tears flowed unchecked beneath her white coif – an admirable reportage of which the photographs still exist – when at last we halted in the middle of a field where some logs smoked rather than burned and a group of civilian evacuees were trying to warm themselves. It was there, at that nightmare bivouac, that I first heard of an exhibition that, Lee said, would have an enormous impact and that the Parisian public, so long deprived of all contact with beauty and elegance, would surely appreciate. It was being prepared with infinite care, though as yet no title had been decided. All that was known was that its whole object was to glorify French fashion and the multiple activities and specialized skills and crafts that centered around it.

The circumstances as much as the setting of our conversation gave an almost surreal character to Lee's descriptions. Unless it was pure provocation on her part.... The Soviet army was at the Oder. Budapest had barely fallen. The Americans had landed at Marseilles. France was in ruins. But in Paris a celebration of the haute couture was being prepared! I advised Lee not to mention any of this at the officers' mess where she was expected. The virtues of elegant living would have no chance of being seen as a priority by her audience there.

One month later, March 28, 1945, the project was realized.
It was the Théâtre de la Mode.

Evening dresses on the 1946 dolls in Anne Surgers' 1990 recreation of the baroque "Grotte Enchantée" set by André Beaurepaire. The youngest of the artists who participated in the Théâtre de la Mode, he was then only twenty years old.

Jean Babilée, the ballet dancer then regarded as genius of the dance incarnate, first revealed to me some of its secrets. We were in Germany. The Allies had just occupied the shores of Lake Constance when we were told to improvise, quickly, a floating stage to receive an entertainment for the troops. That night, at Friedrichshafen, watching Babilée dance, it seemed as if some naked godlike form flew high above the pale waters of the lake. The shortages of the moment explained the lack of costumes.

After the show, in the dugout that served as his dressing room, by the light of a blue-daubed bulb, Babilée recounted what was going on in France. Unimaginable! Paris was waxing enthusiastic over a dreamlike vision, staged and lit by two artists whose names evoked the loveliest moments in the history of ballet: Boris Kochno and Christian Bérard. It was fantastic, an astonishing exhibition where, set in a miniature theater, one saw little people contrived in wire, for lack of anything else available. They were strange, unlikely, difficult to describe, like dolls or small-scale mannequins. Most hallucinatory of all, these so-called dolls were wearing the latest creations of our top couturiers. Moreover, they had real hair, their dresses were made of real material, their minuscule gloves of real leather, their hats real felt, their coats real fur. The reign of ersatz, of detested imitation, something to which the French were so little resigned – had it come to an end? Alas! It was only an illusion, for abundance still lay far ahead. Yet however ephemeral this banishment of the false, it had insolently restored to its place the real, the rare, the beautiful, and the luxurious. And as if part of this audacious dream, Parisians forgot present or past misery and crowded to see these dazzling little figures. They inhabited their own strange little theater world where penury had no place, where it seemed restrictions had disappeared at full speed. Never had the *Pavillon Marsan* known such an attendance. The Théâtre de la Mode was to attract nearly a hundred thousand visitors.

When I returned to Paris, the exhibition had taken off to tour the United States, though now in a slightly different form. New York was to have a first showing of the exhibition in its Spring 1946 version with its thirteen settings and two 237 dolls wearing the latest creations of the haute couture. Milliners, hairdressers, shoemakers, glovemakers, makers of handbags and accessories, as well as jewelers had all conspired to reproduce each designer's inspiration: "with all the delicacy imaginable," as Louise de Vilmorin wrote when, after visiting the Théâtre de la Mode, she was among the first to extoll the seduction of "these little persons clothed in splendor."

The New York public gave the Théâtre de la Mode a triumphal welcome. It had already visited London, Leeds, Barcelona, Stockholm, Copenhagen, and Vienna. Everywhere, reigning sovereigns, royalty, princesses, duchesses, ambassadors and distinguished ladies had disputed the honor of inaugurating this festival that bore the colors of France – the France that some had been too eager to see forgotten and buried. But it seemed neither wan nor pale, this moribund land, while her creative powers appeared more lively than ever! Even before the war was over, the French couture had retrieved the place it had occupied at the International Exhibition of 1937 and it was as if those dark years of defeat and occupation in a torn and suffering Europe might be effaced.

Only another illusion. And yet – was it not the purpose of the theater to create just such an illusion?

In conceiving the Théâtre de la Mode, the Chambre Syndicale de la Couture showed a rare adventurous spirit. And the challenge was great. Let us recapitulate, to brave the miseries of a time where all was obstruction and shortage was no light matter. Today, freed from such preoccupations, are we even capable of being sufficiently amazed? How strange to recall all that in 1990; to evoke a past from which some of us will never truly recover, that past of inventions seized, art abolished, and industry in ruins; a time of empty stomachs, of chapped lips, and shoes in holes; those days of submission and obedience to commands barked out by an invader whose voice was loud and brutal. A bad memory. Better not dwell on it. Forty-five years ago already, and we are told Europe will never again become a breeding ground for barbarism. Germany and its future have become a subject for banal conversation.

A reconstruction, such as that of the Théâtre de la Mode almost half a century after its creation, leads us to evaluate both the merits of those who worked for its success and our capacity for forgetfulness. Among the artists who took part in this adventure are the illustrious and others of whom, apart from their names, we know nothing save that they lived in Paris, worked there, and died there. How could we not wish to fill in these gaps? The least known were often the most innovative.

A special homage must be accorded to two gifted and inventive beings, the first to give the Théâtre de la Mode its modernistic character. In this theater, everything had to be expressed in new terms. Above all, and as quickly as possible, some sort of doll-mannequin had to be devised along fresh lines. A young illustrator of a rather unconventional background, and barely twenty years old, was entrusted with the task of creating the prototype of a small feminine creature, which broke with the conventional mannequins used by the couturiers. This young girl was Eliane Bonabel. Her father by adoption worked for an advertising firm that Robert Ricci employed and was a friend of Céline, the writer. Eliane, at thirteen had been the youngest of Céline's illustrators. To her he had entrusted the illustrations for his *Journey to the End of Night*. She had also created a series of hand-puppets that aroused great interest. Thus it was she who received the commission and her drawings were accepted overnight. Amazement! Shock! Eliane Bonabel had produced a faceless prototype. The head had no place in her sketches. The realization, not easy to execute, was given to a man who had already practiced various means

Eliane Bonabel with one of her dolls in 1945.

of expression. His name was Jean Saint-Martin. The son of a passementerie manufacturer, he had begun to study sculpture, but when in 1915 his father fell on bad times, Jean Saint-Martin was put to work. At sixteen he was engaged by Siegel, the maker of wax mannequins. It was the chance of his lifetime to have such an employer, for in 1920 he participated in what might be called the mannequin revolution for which André Vigneau was responsible and who had a determining influence on the young Jean Saint-Martin. Vigneau, a cellist who had begun by accompanying silent films in the small early cinemas of the poorer quarters, later became a painter, draughtsman, sculptor, and finally a great photographer. It was Vigneau whom Siegel chose to create, for the Decorative Arts Exhibition of 1925, a mannequin "à la garçonne," that boyish, androgynous figure, hair plastered flat, eyebrows plucked, and small heart-shaped mouth. Siegel's mannequins became a symbol of the '20s, giddy years, years of short skirts, knees on show, and the new, free woman. Paris raved over this feminine effigy, which Vigneau had fathered with the help of Jean Saint-Martin. Man Ray's photographs of the Siegel mannequins appeared on the cover of *La Révolution surréaliste*. George Hoyningen-Huene accepted to illustrate the Siegel Company catalogues, and Paul Cuterbridge, with whom Hoyningen-Huene shared a studio, to make a memorable portrait of this new Venus. Jean Saint-Martin had been well schooled. He knew by experience what the phrase "to innovate" implied. At the request of Robert Ricci, alone in his Paris *appartement*, he contrived a small mannequin that was almost an abstraction in its supple lightness. It was immediately accepted. Jean Saint-Martin had made it from wire, twisted, bent, stretched and soldered – wire – a material that was still not too difficult to find in Paris then. Being next commissioned to create one of the sets for the Théâtre de la Mode, more extraordinary still, Saint-Martin made that too, in wire. At its point of departure, the Théâtre de la Mode derived from a well-established custom, dating, some say, from the Middle Ages, when traveling dolls were dispatched far and wide, their mission to present the elegance and prestige of Paris fashion to foreign courts. On seeing to what degree such new fashions could accentuate a woman's charms, numbers of princesses, reassured by the anonymity of such ambassadors, ended by copying their styles. The use of traveling dolls and their purpose of revealing the latest fashions became an exclusively Parisian tradition.

To give new life to an old idea during a period of crisis was all to the credit of the Chambre Syndicale de la Couture Parisienne whose president was Lucien Lelong. But the real instigators of the project, its two dynamos, were Paul Caldaguès, a fashion journalist of exceptional talent, and Robert Ricci. The son of Nina Ricci already had considerable experience behind him. He had been both editor and publicist, a man of communication before his time. He was also a man at once resolute and tactful. When we remember that this was an epoch during which the different couture houses were still imprisoned in a world of prejudice and jealousy, where each was an impregnable fortress set against the other, each supported by a clan of friends, backers, those who inspired

Jean Saint-Martin, creator of mannequins, who made the dolls in wire, used the same material for his "Paris Sketch" décor (page 62).

20

artists, and loyal clients, we must marvel that the strength of an idea or the dynamics of so ambitious a project was enough to weld together all opposing forces into one common enterprise.

Thus the painters of Montmartre collaborated with the decorators of the *beau monde*, while editors of fashion magazines and editors of art books – Michel de Brunhoff at their head – set to and worked together. Adieu old rivalries! The hatchet was buried. Ménilmontant signed a peace treaty with the Place Vendôme, and the slangy accents of some, such as Dignimont – "le grand Dig" as Colette called him – merged with the elaborate affection of others. I hear again the drawn-out alembic phrases of Georges Geffroy who positively intoxicated himself with his near-Proustian pronouncements. But what is in question is not so much the importance of an event that is, after all, only of relative importance, but the significance it has acquired with the passing of time. It could not have been born except in those difficult years of Paris life. A tragic period one will always remember, a haunting period of doubts when the world lived in "the pitiable hope of regaining a lost paradise." Hence those "insensate efforts" of which Aragon spoke, when luxury became part of a prestige to be reconquered. In what other moment of our history could the name of a man like Emilio Terry, gentleman of noble birth, the chosen architect of millionaires, who stemmed from a powerful family of Cuban planters, appear beside that of Joan Rebull, the Catalan sculptor who, in 1937 when the Spanish Republic was proclaimed, was elected to the Parliament of Catalonia? Or that of the somber figure of Douking, who worked like one possessed, wreathed in glory from the recent success of his décors for Giraudoux's Sodom and Gomorrah? Who can tell us

Boris Kochno in the décor by Christian Bérard. Impresario and author of ballets, he was well known for his work with Diaghilev at the Ballets Russes. He was responsible for the lighting of the Théâtre de la Mode.

what he thought of the meteoric rise of a stripling named Beaurepaire, young painter with the air of a schoolboy and twenty-two years his junior – a boy of the wealthy bourgeoisie who, suddenly, at the will of his discoverer, Christian Bérard, was placed on the same level as an artist as acclaimed as he? This mixture of names on the playbill of the Théâtre de la Mode put prewar prodigies such as Cocteau side by side with revelations of the postwar moment such as Beaurepaire. It placed, elbow to elbow, totally contrasting artists. It assembled men who were born with talent, fortune, and influence – Cocteau, Beaurepaire, or Terry – and others who had struggled and tried a thousand métiers before succeeding – men such as Douking, who sang his satirical songs at the cabaret Les Deux-Anes, or

*Eliane Bonabel, who originally imagined and sketched the
prototype of the dolls, accompanied the Théâtre de la
Mode on all its travels.*

André Dignimont in his Palais Royal décor. The Théâtre de la Mode recalled that Paris remained the capital of fashion and that its streets, its gardens, and its atmosphere had never ceased to be a source of inspiration.

Touchagues, assistant to an architect and designer of fabrics. This project brought together Parisians of ancient stock with newcomers: exiles and expatriates like Boris Kochno, the Muscovite; Georges Wakhevitch, Russian citizen of Odessa from Provence; or Grau Sala, Parisian of Catalonia. There were great patrons and protectors of the arts and champions of contemporary music who became linked in friendship with afficionados of the bal musette, while those who were initially to be seen in the tougher quarters of Montmartre suddenly found themselves admitted to the gilded salons of the Faubourg Saint-Germain. Such an extraordinary enterprise could have been orchestrated only by an exceptional artist – Christian Bérard, who became its artistic director. Who could refuse anything to this magician of décor, this charmer, this prince of friendship? None dreamt of thwarting his imaginative flights. The Théâtre de la Mode, the stuff of pure imagination, was also in large part his creation although already he was seeking to distance himself from theatrical work and devote himself to painting. But from that moment, whatever he did or wherever he went, the theater always caught him back. The more the decorator triumphed, the more the painter despaired. We should not dismiss lightly what was a real drama in his life, but, understand the exigencies and purpose of the theater people who demanded Bérard because Bérard was the greatest.

And in that month of March 1945, amid the vast chaos of a devastated France, the triumph of a spectacle that disclosed the ambiguities and the seductions of the epoch was for numerous creators the first sign of a possible survival.

Translated from the French by Lesley Blanch.

Louis Touchagues chose to re-create the Rue de la Paix and the Place Vendôme, one of the most elegant of Parisian settings.

August 1944: euphoria in the streets of a capital given over to the joy of its liberation. Lee Miller, American, photographer, and war correspondent, arrived in Paris with the Allied troops. She had been a well-known figure on the Paris scene in the 1930s.

As the War Ended

Herbert R. Lottman

Looking back at that intoxicating moment when French-flagged tanks under General Leclerc roared through the streets of Paris, followed soon enough by Allied troops who had reached France via the Normandy beaches, one can almost hear the collective sigh of relief. Resistance journalist Albert Camus expressed it while it was happening: "On the warmest and loveliest of August nights the everlasting stars in the Paris sky mix with tracer bullets, the smoke from fires, and the multicolored rockets of the people's joy," he wrote on the front page of *Combat*, the daily newspaper, which only that week had burst out of clandestinity. "This matchless night sees the end of four years of monstrous history and indescribable struggle during which France came to grips with its shame and its fury." This appeared on August 25, the day Free France's chief General Charles de Gaulle arrived in liberated Paris to receive the act of surrender signed by the German commandant, General Dietrich von Choltitz. On the following day de Gaulle and members of his provisional government marched from the Arc de Triomphe to the Place de la Concorde along the Champs Elysées; later they paid their respects to Notre Dame, and no matter that sporadic shooting accompanied their triumph. How natural it was that some Parisians reacted by tearing up the ration tickets that had governed their lives during the long years of war and occupation.[1]

How natural, and how unwise. For the autumn and the winter that followed the liberation of Paris – the months during which the Théâtre de la Mode was conceived and elaborated – were in many ways the harshest of all the war – the weather brutal, the shortages acute. A full sixteen months later, in December 1945, bread rationing was put into effect once more, the daily allowance decreased. "How can one live with 300 grams of bread per day," complained the cantankerous chronicler Paul Léautaud, "when food is already so rare?"[2] The summertime Liberation had begun so well. Before the end of August 1944 the Paris Stock Exchange had reopened, as had a couple of cinema houses (if only to show newsreels). In early September it was announced that horse racing was to start; theaters were drawing crowds. The persistent fine weather, the discovery of supplies left by the fleeing enemy, the generosity of American soldiers, encouraged a certain euphoria.[3] Attention could be turned to dealing with the consequences of four years of enemy occupation, and notably to settling accounts with fellow Frenchmen accused of political or economic collaboration with the Germans. Purge courts began to function even before the provisional government took full possession of French territory, and as major cities and districts were liberated, a network of special courts was installed to deal with officials and private citizens accused of collusion with the Nazis. Soon a High Court was ready to hear the cases of members of the Vichy government, even of Marshal Pétain himself (who turned himself in at the Swiss frontier on April 25, 1945).

Some of the first purge trials concerned well-known political activists and writers who had dominated the front pages of German-occupied Paris, and there were some swift sentences of death by firing squad.[4] All this while Charles de Gaulle and his ministers – still provisional – drew up plans for election on the municipal level (April-May 1945), for county leadership (September), and then for a national Constituent Assembly (in

A member of the FFI (Forces Françaises de l'Intérieur), the organization which gave the signal for the insurrection of Paris, August 19, 1944.

October), this last responsible for the writing of a constitution for the Fourth Republic. In October 1944, the month when the Chambre Syndicale de la Couture Parisienne and charities represented by l'Entraide Française drew up plans for their cooperative effort, it did seem as if a return to normality was possible. Indeed, it was in the first week of October that leading fashion houses resumed regular seasonal showings. In the words of the communiqué of the Chambre Syndicale: "Prepared during a period of incredible material difficulties, these new fashion shows, offering a reduced number of models, are the result of a tremendous collective effort, and demonstrate the desire of Parisian fashion houses to lead the way to a rapid recovery of the national economy" (*Le Figaro*, October 3). The October 11 *Le Figaro* cited a calendar of thirty-five collections.

At the same time the press was headlining the reopening of cinemas (starting on October 13), even if at first there was to be only one showing each evening, five days a week, a Saturday matinée and two on Sunday. Parisians also learned that electricity distribution was improving day by day. On October 9 electricity was available to Parisians by 6:00 p.m., with the promise that they could hope for current as early as 5:30 p.m. in the following days (*Combat*, October 10). That month Parisians had a choice of no fewer than thirty-nine theaters (including the Comédie-Française, Odéon, Opéra-Comique, Ambigu, Marigny, Mogador, and Palais-Royal), of fifteen vaudeville houses (including Bobino, Casino de Paris, Lido, Mayol, and Tabarin), and three circuses.[5] Yet soon the shorter autumn days, the approach of winter, confronted Parisians with the realization that deprivations were not behind them. "Freezing of material supplies – store shelves are empty; nothing to sell even with ration tickets," their newspapers told them. "Manufacturers aren't manufacturing. Those who possess cloth are waiting for the devaluation of the franc before releasing it, unless they are obliged to" (*L'Aube*, November 19-20, 1944). Would Paris again become the City of Light? The question was raised; the answer was: not before the end of hostilities – the final defeat of Germany. But American military authorities saw no reason why street lights could not be turned on – suitably dimmed, and ready to be switched off during air raid warnings (*L'Aube*, November 24). And would Paris get its buses back? Not yet; the subway would have to do (*L'Aube*, November 28). "Where to find shoes?" Rationing had disappeared, but so had shoes, even wooden-soled shoes. In truth, the press had to admit, there was a black market for those who could afford to pay for new shoes (*L'Aube*, November 30). Speaking to the French by radio on

November 19, General de Gaulle confessed that much remained to be done to restore France's political, economic, and military powers. Only half as much coal was being produced as before the war. Raw materials weren't going to factories because of the priority given to the war effort (*L'Aube*, November 21).

It would have taken more than a radio talk to deal with the complex circumstances that were making peacetime life so much like wartime. There was of course the fact that the French were living under an exceptional political regime. There had been a prewar Republic whose democratic institutions were suspended and then abolished by Pétain's Etat Française in Vichy. La France Libre, and its chief, General de Gaulle, received its mandate only from patriotic conviction. Under the Germans and Vichy, hapless French men and women had seen much of what they produced go to feed Hitler's war machine. Factories worked for the enemy, and production of vital goods went to pay the stiff indemnities levied on France under the terms of the 1940 armistice. Now a Free France was obliged to marshal its own resources, its hands and its tools, to pursue the war (which would of course end with German capitulation only the following May), and to reconstruct roads and bridges and factories to assure postwar recovery.

The paradoxical result was that even more of a sacrifice was to be demanded of French citizens in the immediate postwar than in any of the grim years that preceded it. Let statistics tell the story. Infant mortality had risen at the outbreak of war: From 6.4 percent in 1939 it reached 8.6 percent in 1940, declining to 7 percent in 1941, 7.4 percent in 1942, 7.8 percent in 1943, 7.9 percent in 1944, but then soared to 10.9 percent in 1945, a function of shortage and poor quality of milk and other farm produce, as well as chaotic distribution.[6] Production of coal – the most striking index of comfort and hardship of the post-Liberation months – declined at the end of the Occupation, in millions of metric tons falling from 42,427 tons in 1943 to 26,577 tons the following year (before the war consumption had been 52,820 tons).[7]

The production of other essential goods followed the same curve. With 100 as the pre-war index, textiles were turned out at the rate of 29 in 1942, 23 in 1943, 14 in 1944. The index for leather during these years was 41, 36, 25.[8] A chief cause was the paralysis of transportation – inoperative railway lines, the shortage of freight cars, the destruction of canal locks through which coal barges passed. While most factories survived the war, the raw materials needed in manufacturing had all but disappeared. The advancing Allies, and the retreating Germans, had systematically destroyed harbors, bridges, and railroad infrastructure. All the bridges across the Seine from Paris to the sea, as well as the Loire bridges from Nevers to the sea, and the Rhone's from Lyon to the sea, were gone. One hundred and fifteen

In spite of all of the difficulties under the Occupation, Parisian women made every effort, as reported in Vogue USA, November 1, 1944, to maintain the "nice neat 'quand même' appearance."

main railroad stations and twenty-four main marshaling yards had been destroyed or seriously damaged. On canals and riverways 282 locks had been rendered inoperative, 3,000 barges destroyed; some 5,200 kilometers of navigable waterways (of the total 9,600) were closed to traffic. Of 17,000 steam locomotives possessed by French railroads in 1939, only 2,900 were then running, and only half of the 460,000 freight cars.[9]

A part of the problem, all the same, was psychological. Personal energies had simply been demobilized by the disappearance of the enemy, and there was a feeling among rank-and-file Frenchmen that supplies from the United States and elsewhere would soon be flooding France. (Indeed, as late as March 1945 President Franklin D. Roosevelt told Americans that they would have to tighten their belts until the end of the war to help nations threatened with famine. In fact, the United States was then trying to deal with the pressing needs of all war victim nations and could not reasonably satisfy all the needs of one of them.) One factor could be quantified: there were up to one million men in the army and auxiliary resistance forces, and about two million men (and women) were believed to be in camps and detention centers in Germany. For those present and available to work, inadequate food reduced their productive capabilities.[10] A year later – in March 1946 – the press was able to say that Parisians were surviving on 1,400 calories a day, fewer than during the Occupation, fewer – so they believed – than defeated Berliners were receiving (*L'Aurore*, March 17-19, 1946).

Image of wartime: old means of locomotion are back in service and sometimes it is a woman who fills the role of coachman.

It is tempting to try to imagine life in Paris as it was in the weeks during which the Théâtre de la Mode took concrete form, to stand in the wings as the artists and their teams created mannequins and décors in that first winter of free Paris – a winter during which the war continued to be fought on parcels of French soil. For if Metz in Lorraine and Strasbourg in Alsace were liberated by the end of November 1944, fierce fighting continued in eastern France through the New Year. There was a German counter-offensive in the Ardennes, and the Allies were even readying themselves to abandon Strasbourg after its liberation, something General de Gaulle refused to accept (Strasbourg was held, but with French troops). The enemy still held Colmar to the south, with a pocket of surrounding territory. On the Atlantic coast, another pocket of German resistance in Royan was mopped up in April 1945; but St. Nazaire, La Rochelle, Lorient, and Brest remained in the possession of the enemy until

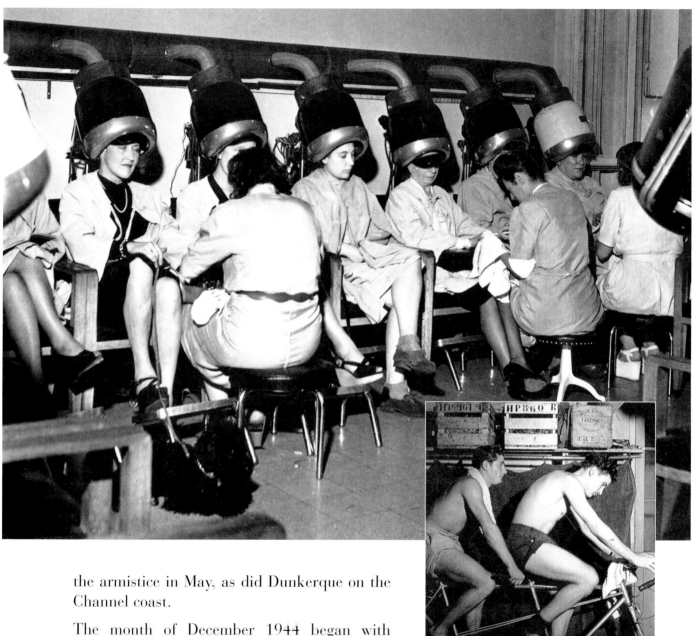

the armistice in May, as did Dunkerque on the Channel coast.

The month of December 1944 began with reports of the continued shortage of clothing. Wasn't it possible, one newspaper demanded of the government, to release sufficient materials so that people could at least get the stockings and socks and handkerchiefs they so much needed? (*L'Aube*, December 2). Then good news came from traditional British colonial suppliers of wool: A significant allotment of this precious material was promised to France (*L'Aube*, December 3-4). "It's been four years since Frenchmen have been able to buy new

How to remain well-coiffed when hairdryers no longer work for lack of electricity? Parisian hairdresser Gervais became a star when he rigged his dryers to stove pipes leading to a furnace supplied by fans turned by relays of young men on stationary tandem bicycles in the basement. The chain gang in the service of pincurls pedaled the equivalent of 320 kilometers a day, drying about half that many heads.

underwear," complained a popular daily, which predicted that citizens would soon be "naked" (*Le Figaro*, December 6). Then there was more good news for Christmas: Thread was on its way! Two ration tickets could be handed in for two grams of silk or six grams of other material (*L'Aube*, December 26). Yet it was going to be a winter, as the papers reported candidly, "without coal, without wood, without gas, without electricity, without shoes, and without clothing" (*Le Figaro*, December 30). "Bread has become bad again," noted cranky Paul Léautaud. "Noodles are like paste. Dried vegetables have to be dried. Sugar doesn't melt. Cheese can't be found. Butter rations are microscopic. Oil unknown, tobacco still restricted. Coffee and chocolate are no longer seen in public."[11]

Like most of his fellows, Léautaud had his mind on his dwindling supply of coal. At the beginning of December the Ministry of Industrial Production set up twenty investigatorial units to look for hidden stocks of coal; public agencies were forbidden to use coal for heating before January 1 (*L'Aube*, December 1). In the middle of December the provisional government nationalized the coal mines of northern France. It was the first such nationalization, an indication of how essential coal was for national recovery as well as for comfort and health; it was also a function of the increasing demands of workers, and of the demands by the Resistance generation for a purge of prewar management. Soon Renault automobiles and Air France were also nationalized.[12]

With the New Year, Minister of Information Pierre-Henri Teitgen warned fellow Frenchmen that "1945 will be the hardest year of all, that of the final stretch," but he also proclaimed it "the year of hope."[13] The moment can be seized in the diary of the caustic journalist Jean Galtier-Boissière, who kept a day-by-day chronicle of events. Contemporary accounts such as his remind us that Parisians celebrated the New Year in an atmosphere of war, with its daily quota of heroism at the front but also of treason at home – often followed by swift punishment (sometimes, so Galtier-Boissière seemed to feel, too swift to be just). There was the realization, and the fear, that victory was not yet certain; there was talk of German secret weapons; it was thought that Hitler's Berchtesgaden redoubt could hold out for years...[14] This diarist was less than enthusiastic about the Resistance men in charge of the nation, who may have known how to blow up trains but did not necessarily know how to make them run.[15] In his lively journal we can almost visualize the snow as it falls and freezes in January 1945. It seemed as if there had never been as much snow in Paris, and it had to happen in the very year when coal was sorely lacking. "Who would have believed it? This sixth winter of the war in the liberated capital is the hardest of all for Parisians: neither coal nor wood, with unusually cold weather and snowstorms to torment us."[16] Snowed in, the writer Colette told a correspondent: "I am burning everything I have left, and live under the covers with a hot water bottle."[17]

Rationing was as ubiquitous as it had ever been. *Combat*, for example, published a two-column listing of what French families could expect to have on their tables during January. One still needed tickets in order to buy bread, flour, fats. The weekly ration of meat amounted to 180 to 250 grams depending on one's age and activity; cheese was

The Trocadéro under snow during the winter of 1944-1945, one of the coldest Paris had known in a long time. The icy streets were deserted, and people shivered in unheated apartments; coal deliveries were more difficult than ever.

33

limited to 20 grams a week regardless of category. Sugar, chocolate, and candy were also measured out, and those who made a case for extra amounts of dairy products for health reasons were required to give up their right to wine (December 23, 1944). Ration tickets didn't tell the whole story, for stores often lacked even rationed goods.[18] More restrictions in mid-January: there would be no gas in the evenings, no electricity during the day (except at lunchtime). Travel by steam locomotive was banned.[19]

At that moment writer Léautaud went to see Charlie Chaplin's *The Gold Rush* in an unheated cinema and came out of it with icy feet. When a companion observed that the snow and cold were said to be coming from America, grouchy Léautaud snapped: "That's something else we owe them."[20] The next day he recorded the outside temperature as 16° F. Freezing, ill-nourished, living by the light of his candles, Léautaud saw his last logs disappear into the fireplace. "Everything is worse than during the Occupation," he grunted – thinking also of the purge trials that were threatening many of his friends.[21] We also have the testimony of Simone de Beauvoir, who, with Jean-Paul Sartre, decided that "Materially, the situation had worsened since the previous year."[22] When it became really cold, Sartre went around with an old sheepskin jacket that was shedding its wool; she was able to buy a rabbit-hair coat for herself from a fellow war prisoner of Sartre's, and except for one black suit that she saved for important outings, she had only old clothes to wear, and continued to walk on shoes with wooden soles. The crisis, they discovered, was even affecting the production line of literature, the arts.[23]

Some of the amenities of peacetime were taken away again. Horse racing was suspended; shop window lights were forbidden. Newspapers were obliged to publish in a reduced format.[24] "The French people, especially in large cities, are suffering cruelly from the cold, and most of them are receiving insufficient food," explained General de Gaulle in a radio speech on January 17, 1945. "Countless homes are absolutely without fuel. In nearly all workshops, offices, and stores, people work without heating. Hospitals, day-care centers, and schools are receiving a minimum amount of fuel... There is barely enough milk for young children and the ill... Our agriculture, while in relatively better condition, nevertheless lacks fertilizer and equipment that would allow it to make the progress of which it is capable. Our devastated cities and villages are managing to clear away their ruins, but lack everything they need to begin reconstruction."[25] There were flashes of optimism, all the same. On January 21 large quantities of cotton were reported en route from Chad, with more promised aid from the mills of England. Before the month was over, ration tickets were validated for six grams of cotton thread (*L'Aurore*, January 21 and 25).

It was only at the beginning of 1945, with an issue dated January-February, that the industry showcase journal *L'Officiel de la Couture* reappeared with issue number 276. The previous issue, number 275, had been published in August 1944 before the Liberation; indeed, *L'Officiel* had not ceased to appear during the months of combat that followed the Allied landings in Normandy. Now, with the war carried to enemy territory, there was scarcely an allusion to it; readers would have to wait until the July-August 1945 issue for reference to material difficulties. The point, as an editorial in October made clear, was to smile in hard times. For details, one had to turn to American reports on the French fashion industry. In its first report on Parisian styles since the fall of France, American *Vogue* noted, in the October 15, 1944, issue: "Whereas the clothes made during the German occupation were intended by the various dressmakers to be deliberately fancy and exaggerated, in order to taunt the Germans, now Paris feels that she is part of the war again. Once any saving of material or labor only benefited the Germans. Now everything is changed…" In a message to *Vogue* on November 15, Lucien Lelong, as president of the Fashion Couture Association, described the restrictions designers were observing (40 models per collection instead of 150; only half the models in fabrics containing 30 percent wool; strict limitations on the amount of material that went into each dress, suit, coat). The January 15, 1945, *Vogue* portrayed the well-dressed Parisian woman with a bicycle, explaining: "When you go to dine with friends in Paris, you go by Métro or bicycle, and you usually bring along a share of the dinner…"

Early in February Colette was able to assure well-wishers that she had a fire going. She could not say that it was much of a fire or that she'd still have it in a week's time, but she did have one. The weather was warming up, in any case. The writer, arthritic and virtually bed-ridden, had been getting food parcels from friends in the provinces during and since the German occupation; now she reported that her husband had made a trip to the country and returned with a dozen eggs and a hare. But she had no more coffee than anyone else![26] Punctilious diarist Galtier-Boissière watches as prices soar for sponges, bicycles, typewriters, men's suits, even plants and flowers; discovers a thriving black market in Métro stations for chocolate and tobacco; and listens to French traitors broadcast-

The Place Vendôme, in front of the house of Schiaparelli, a mannequin (model) with Schiaparelli workers. In spite of the fabric shortages, the haute couture managed to maintain its creativity during the war and to provide jobs for couture personnel.

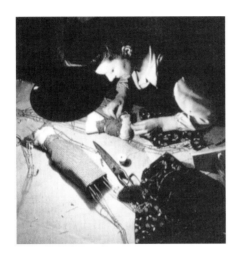

In the couture workrooms, cutting, fitting, and sewing for the dolls of the Théâtre de la Mode. Workers of furs and their sewing machines often moved to several different parts of Paris in one day, depending on where electricity was on.

ing appeals for desertion.[27] Late in February Supply Minister Paul Ramadier admitted that shortages were not about to end. Among the insoluble problems, in the short run: Livestock, inadequately nourished during the years of occupation, had not been renewed. Producers resisted delivery of their goods; the black market became the most reliable supplier. France needed 15,000 freight cars a week and never had more than 8,700 since Christmas.[28] "Take care of your clothing," the press advised – as if in the middle of the war. The clothing industry was at a virtual standstill. One must not expect a new wool suit until...1946 (*L'Aube*, February 22). At the beginning of March 1945, when the costumes and mannequins and scenery for the Théâtre de la Mode were getting feverish last-minute touches in studios and workshops scattered about Paris, Charles de Gaulle stood before the Assemblée Consultative to offer a progress report on the first six months of his administration. "The fog has barely lifted," he admitted; the grave nature of France's situation was only now becoming clear. "From the economic point of view the serious damage done to vital centers and to communications, the destruction of three-quarters of our means of transportation, the utilization for military needs of two-thirds of what remains to us, the almost total lack of imports, the wiping out of stocks prevent or at least hamper the activity of a large number of enterprises, keep 400,000 people out of work and cause partial unemployment to one million two hundred thousand others, making the supplying of large cities a continual tour de force, delaying the recovery of agricultural production." He had never claimed, added de Gaulle, that everything would suddenly become perfect in a nation that possessed only a third of the coal needed by its industry, to say nothing of the coal needed to heat homes.

But there had been no civil war, he pointed out, and some had feared that there might be one as the Gaullists took over from the Pétainists. Priority had been given to winning the war, and those who made sacrifices now contributed to that. He had, General de Gaulle reminded his fellow citizens, restored basic freedoms, and even extended them – by giving women the right to vote for the first time in France.[29]

The war went on. When the Théâtre de la Mode opened its doors in March 1945, six Allied armies were pushing deeper into Germany; one result was the liberation of French war prisoners, and of young Frenchmen working in German factories. In April it was the return of the *déportés*, and France discovered the depths of horror of the concentration camp inferno, a revelation that was to reopen scarcely healed wounds, providing a new *raison d'être* for the prosecution of fellow citizens accused of collaborating with the enemy. The war also meant, for the clothing industry, the filling of orders for 2.5 million uniforms (*L'Aurore*, March 2).

On the very day that the Théâtre de la Mode was inaugurated, diarist Paul Léautaud recorded a personal and less happy experience. He had an appointment with a friend's dressmaker and brought with him a piece of material the heiress Florence Gould had given him (not the good prewar quality, but a mix of wool and cotton). The dressmaker couldn't help him, so he went on to a tailor on the Rue de Grenelle who had already made the coat he was wearing, now "threadbare and full of holes." Could a coat be made from Madame Gould's gift? The tailor pointed out that his cloth wasn't everything; he also needed canvas backing, buttons, a lining... Did Léautaud have all of that? Of course, he did not. How much would it cost, the work and the missing supplies? Four thousand francs. Léautaud wrapped up his fabric and said thank you. It was hard enough to be able to afford the food he needed. He'd have them put patches on his old coat, even if the color wasn't a perfect match.[30]

We know something the organizers of the Théâtre de la Mode could not have known when they set their dates: Their show – scheduled to close in Paris on May 10 – was to outlast the war in Europe. But a happy ending wasn't obvious during the run of the event. On April 4 women's shoes, even bedroom slippers, were back on the list of rationed goods. Meat was to remain scarce, newspaper readers learned, for another three months (*L'Aurore*, April 5 and 12, 1945). "If they had told us," an exasperated Galtier-Boissière scribbled in his diary, "that eight months after the Liberation we'd have less of everything than during the Occupation, we'd never have believed it..."[31] One could not even look toward the front for relief. Galtier-Boissière was reliably informed, by a general staff officer "who is close to the sun," that the Germans were prepared to resist for another year...[32]

Paris is free but the war is not over. Nor are the shortages. For lack of gasoline, bicycles and horses and carriages will be part of life for a long time to come.

The evening of the inauguration of the Théâtre de la Mode, in front of the Geffroy décor. From left to right: Lucien Lelong, president of the Chambre Syndicale de la Couture; Robert Ricci, head of the Commission for Press and Public Relations of the same organization; Madame Lanvin, the minister of industrial production; Robert Lacoste; and Georges Geffroy.

1. Alfred Sauvy, *La Vie économique des Français de 1939 à 1945* (Paris: Flammarion, 1978), 221.
2. Paul Léautaud, *Journal littéraire XVI* (Paris: Mercure de France, 1946), 312-13.
3. Raymond Ruffin, *La Vie des Français au jour le jour de la Libération à la victoire* (Paris: Presses de la Cité, 1986), 20-25, 45-58.
4. Herbert R. Lottman, *The Purge* (New York: Morrow, 1986), 132-41.
5. Ruffin, 85.
6. Sauvy, 190, 224-25.
7. Ibid., 153.
8. Ibid., 155.
9. *L'Anneé politique (de la Libération de Paris au 31 décembre 1945)* (Paris: Le Grand Siècle, 1946), 15-16.
10. Ibid., 18.
11. Léautaud, 163.
12. *L'Anneé politique*, 76-82.
13. Ibid., 90.
14. Jean Galtier-Boissière, *Mon journal depuis la Libération* (Paris: La Jeune Parque, 1945), 108, 130.
15. Ibid., 111.
16. Ibid., 113, 122, 130.
17. Colette, *Lettres à ses pairs* (Paris: Flammarion, 1978), 138.
18. Ruffin, 122.
19. *Combat*, January 14-15, 1945, in Ruffin, 124.
20. Léautaud, 175.
21. Ibid., 176-77.
22. Simone de Beauvoir, *La Force des choses* (Paris: Gallimard, 1963), 21.
23. Ibid.
24. Ruffin, 125.
25. Ibid., 126.
26. Marie-Thérèse Colléaux, "Six Lettres de Colette aux petites fermières," *Cahiers Colette 10* (St. Sauveur en Puisaye, Yonne: Société des Amis de Colette, 1988), 31-32.
27. Galtier-Boissière, 144, 153, 158.
28. *L'Anneé politique*, 115-16.
29. Ibid., 442-46.
30. Léautaud, 211-12.
31. Galtier-Boissière, 209.
32. Ibid., 215.

The eve of the inauguration of the Théâtre de la Mode:
general mobilization and feverish trips between the
couturier workrooms and the Pavillon Marsan.

The Théâtre de la Mode: Birth and Rebirth

Stanley Garfinkel

The story of the Théâtre de la Mode concerns fashion, theater, and the haute couture beginning to recapture its place of eminence in the world. It is also about a particularly French phenomenon: the alliance of fashion designers and artists working together, in this case to create a touching and poetic symbol of hope and renewal.

Paris had just been liberated after four years of German occupation, but the war continued and conditions of life became even more difficult. "The Liberation was a gigantic *fête*, but afterwards we returned to reality...we rediscovered economic reality."[1]

The national economy lay in ruins. Above all, there was human devastation. Aside from the dead, the wounded, and the deported, some five million men, women, and children were without adequate shelter, food, or clothing.

The organization responsible for providing and coordinating war relief was L'Entraide Française. In the fall of 1944 its president, Raoul Dautry, called on his friend Robert Ricci at the Chambre Syndicale de la Haute Couture Parisienne.[2] "He had had the idea of asking the Chambre Syndicale to organize something which would show the continuing vitality of the fashion industries and the couture and which, at the

Left:
From sketch to materialization: in his workroom Jean Saint-Martin working on the wire structures of the dolls.

Right:
With Eliane Bonabel, drilling a hole in the plaster head, which will fit onto a wire stem at the neck.

same time, would prove that they were very concerned about the fate of those in need and were willing to make a great effort to help them."[3]

The idea was discussed and approved at an executive meeting of the Chambre Syndicale under the presidency of Lucien Lelong. Robert Ricci, head of the Commission of Press and Public Relations of the Chambre Syndicale, was placed in charge of the project with the help of Paul Caldaguès, Délégué Général. According to Robert Ricci, it was Paul Caldaguès who first suggested an exhibition of dolls dressed by the couture houses but, they decided, the occasion required a new and exciting kind of doll. Robert Ricci therefore asked the young artist Eliane Bonabel to make some sketches.

"We immediately thought that these dolls should not be too solid as this would be reminiscent of a toy. I thought of something transparent...my point of departure was the tables of measurements found in fashion magazines at that time."[4] Eliane Bonabel's sketches of a 27.5-inch wire figurine were approved by the Chambre Syndicale and it was decided to ask the refugee Catalan sculptor Rebull to create plaster heads so that the miniature mannequins could have real coiffures and hats to complete the costumes. "Above all Rebull asked that his heads not have makeup...they should be small sculptures..."[5]

Ricci and Caldaguès wanted the most prominent Parisian artists of the moment to be associated with the project. The obvious choice as art director was Christian (Bébé) Bérard, an artist of versatility, talent, wit, and charm and a favorite of Parisian fashionable, artistic, theatrical, and literary circles. Bérard called upon his friends: ballet impresario Boris Kochno; writer, poet, filmmaker Jean Cocteau; painters Dignimont, Douking, Grau-Sala, Touchagues; stage designers Wakhevitch and Malclès; sculptor Jean Saint-Martin who specialized in objects made of wire; decorator Georges Geffroy; and a new, young talent in Paris, twenty-year-old André Beaurepaire.

It was Robert Ricci who solved the problem of how to present the dolls and allow each artist his own place in the sun. "It was I who had the idea...of a little theater in which [each artist] would build his set...and we would place in them the dolls dressed by the couturiers. And it was then that I thought we should name it the 'Théâtre de la Mode.'"[6]

The artists and couturiers were given complete freedom to create the sets and the clothes they pleased. Bérard decided his décor would represent a theater-opera house. The others chose morning, afternoon, or evening scenes so that the proper variety of clothes could be shown in a corresponding environment. Each couture house, according to the size and nature of its collection – some were specialized in tailoring or sportswear, others made clothes for all hours of the day – agreed to produce from one to five outfits.

During the winter of 1944-1945 the Théâtre de la Mode gradually took shape. The clothes were miniature versions of the full-sized collection. Each was fashioned with the same precision and perfection as the original: tiny hand-stitched buttonholes for hand-covered buttons that could really be unbuttoned, pockets that were really pockets, inner construction as meticulously finished as if the dress were to be worn inside out.

Right and below right:
The miniaturization of clothes and accessories for the 27.5-inch dolls was carried out to the smallest detail both inside and out. Some shoes had contrasting trim one millimeter wide, handbags opened and had completely fitted interiors.

Below left:
The Théâtre de la Mode also called upon the great milliners of Paris, as hats at that time were perhaps the single most important fashion accessory. Under the picture hats, boaters, and evening egrets, the hair had been coiffed by means of tiny pins and hair-rollers specially made to the scale of the dolls.

The stripes of Carven's "Sucre d'Orge" were too wide to be used for the mini version, "so we reduced them by cutting the fabric and resewing it."[7] At Patou a special basketweave fabric was remade to scale.

Plagued by inadequate heating, electricity cuts, barely adequate food rations, and often obliged to get to work on foot or on bicycles, the skilled tailors and seamstresses in the workrooms of the couturiers and milliners nevertheless threw themselves into the project with enthusiasm and fervor. At first, the figurines were only to be dressed, hatted, and coiffed. "But later there was a kind of rivalry between the couture houses and they said 'Why not have shoes?' So then little shoes were made. 'Why not have bags?' 'Why not have umbrellas?' A few workrooms even made underwear. It would never be seen, but it amused them. You have no idea of the competition between the couturiers. Each one tried to find out what the other was doing in order to do more and better."[8]

All the artisans who worked with the couture houses became involved. Tiny belts, flowers, gloves, feather ornaments for evening coiffures, miniature embroideries and jewelry were created to complement each costume. The great coiffeurs of the era such as Antoine and Guillaume create coiffures to scale.

The challenge of creating miniature hats for the Théâtre de la Mode is recounted by milliner Claude Saint-Cyr. "For a dress the measurements are very important, but for a hat they must be correct to a millimeter. A little too far forward, a little too far back and it's finished – it no longer flatters the face. We needed tiny moulds, it was a work of precision which gave us a great deal of trouble...we fitted, we cut, we repinned, we started again..."[9]

The furs worn by some of the figurines had specific problems of their own. "Insignificant things took on great importance. The machines [to sew the pelts] needed needles. The needles came from Germany. Where could we find needles? We needed colored thread, so we bought white or natural thread and dyed it. Our workrooms were cold, the electricity cuts constant... Plying a needle, working a skin, wetting a skin in freezing water, was terrible..."[10]

There were shortages of every conceivable kind. The Chambre Syndicale had to obtain special government permits for the lumber and plywood used for the décors. Madame Raymonde Scheikevitch (then Madame Robert Ricci) remembers finally locating a supply of plaster for the heads and delivering it to the workshop in her little gazogene runabout. The couturiers ransacked their stocks for scraps of fabric. The crimson velvet for the decoration was rented from Belloir & Jallot, furnishers for receptions and exhibitions.

In order to increase the profits for L'Entraide Française, Robert Ricci used all his powers of persuasion. Each artist donated his services. The couture houses not only contributed labor and material but also made a financial contribution for each costume and hat provided for the exhibition. Even the company that printed the programs did so at no profit. A prestigious locale, the Grand Gallery of the *Pavillon Marsan* at the Museum of Decorative Arts, was secured at no cost. All revenue from the sales of tickets and programs went to L'Entraide Française and sales of cloth dolls dressed by the couturiers were to bring in additional profits.

Shortly before opening day, the décors were delivered to the *Pavillon Marsan*. "Bérard decided to decorate his on the spot, to paint the false marble and the caryatides himself...it was my first experience on a set in construction and it was fabulous to watch Bérard, Cocteau, and all the others at work..."[11]

When the figurines were placed in their décors there were a few unpleasant surprises. "They [the dolls] were impeccable in the

Christian Bérard at work on his decor, "Le Théâtre," which he insisted on painting himself.

couture houses but once in the décors suddenly it could be seen that the proportions were not right...and they were taken back to the workrooms. There was a heated discussion about the height of the heels for the shoes...they were all wrong...everyone was a bit worked up..."[12] "And little by little the sets came to life. The last day when they were lit, and all these mysterious places took on their own autonomy, it was magical."[13]

The exhibition opened the evening of March 27, 1945. The Garde Républicaine in helmets and uniform flanked the stairs leading to the Grand Gallery. "It was one of those particularly Parisian *fêtes*...the *'Tout-Paris'* was there: Marie-Blanche de Polignac, Louise de Vilmorin, Marie-Laure de Noailles – all the leaders of Paris society."[14] "...all the necessary pomp, the music of Henri Sauguet, it was an enchantment."[15] "The public walked almost in silence, religiously. The *Pavillon Marsan* is immense, an enormous room entirely hung in crimson velvet. The theaters were the only sources of light, lit only by the lights of their ramps."[16]

Day after day, the people of Paris, starved for beauty, for glamour, for amusement after four years of occupation, streamed to the *Pavillon Marsan*. Students came to sketch and to study how the fabric had been cut and draped. So did fashion-conscious Parisiennes who made their own clothes or had them made by *petites couturières* but who might never go to a collection themselves. (It must be remembered that ready-to-wear as we know it today did not exist in France at that time.)

As well as the Théâtre de la Mode, there was also an exhibition of historic French fashion drawings arranged by French *Vogue's* Editor-in-Chief Michel de Brunhoff and displayed in kiosks designed by Pierre Boucher.[17] On the walls, attached by pins in the shape of tiny winged hands, symbols of the Paris Couture, was a display about the couture industry and its workers.

The exhibition was so successful that it was prolonged for several weeks. At its conclusion, receipts for l'Entraide Française came to about a million francs.[18] It had also had its uses for the couture industry. "Something which had continued to exist but which was not known to all had reappeared in the mainstream of life. One might have thought that the couture was a bygone thing which was going to disappear or which had already disappeared. On the contrary, I think there were 100,000 visitors to the Théâtre de la Mode, and these 100,000 people who had paid their entrance fee, who had paid for a program, spread the news that there was still a flowering of fashion houses and that they were still there to defend French fashion."[19]

The Théâtre de la Mode was still on exhibition May 8, 1945, when the war ended. That very day Raoul Dautry, by now minister of reconstruction and urbanism of the Provisional Government, wrote to the French ambassador in London, René Massigli: "I am writing to ask you to do everything you can to help the Syndicat de la Mode and the *Daily Mail* to set up in London the exhibition of the Théâtre de la Mode which has had a brilliant success in Paris and which has brought in more than a million francs for L'Entraide Française... France has little, alas, to export, but she has her appreciation of beautiful things and the skill of her couture houses..."[20]

The British called it "The Fantasy of Fashion." It opened in London September 12, 1945, at the Prince's Gallery. Inaugurated by the Duchess of Kent and Madame Massigli, for the benefit of the R.A.F. Benevolent Fund and L'Entraide Française, it was the first foreign exhibition to visit London since the outbreak of World War II. A private viewing was arranged for Her Majesty Queen Elizabeth. In six weeks some 120,000 Londoners queued up to exclaim over the extraordinary fashions from Paris. Restrictions on textiles had been very severe in wartime Britain and were still in force. British women were still either in uniform or wearing shabby, skimpy, utilitarian clothes. They must have had very mixed feelings about this French extravaganza, but it did enable them to dream of a more glamorous future.

On January 2, 1946, the Théâtre de la Mode opened in Leeds, center of Yorkshire's textile industry and an important prewar source of fabric for the French fashion industry. Comments in the visitors book reflected its success: "Paris transferred bodily to Leeds," "Thank you, Paris," "Even better than the publicity," "Indescribably lovely."

Elements of the Théâtre de la Mode had been sent to Barcelona in the summer of 1945 as part of a larger French exhibition. During the fall and winter of 1945-1946 portions of it had toured Copenhagen, Stockholm, and Vienna. In Denmark the king and queen

Above:
London, September 1945: Madame Massigli, wife of the French ambassador to London, and the Duchess of Kent in front of the décor by Louis Touchagues.

Left, top and bottom:
The evening of the inauguration at the Pavillon Marsan: flanked by the Garde Républicaine, mannequins greeted the visitors with the program of the exhibition. The decorators had worked until the very last moment, leaving just as the official personalities arrived (from left to right: Robert Ricci, Boris Kochno, Christian Bérard, Lucien Lelong).

visited the exhibition, in Stockholm the crown prince and princess. Everywhere newspaper headlines acclaimed the continued vitality of French taste and skills.

In the spring of 1946 the Chambre Syndicale decided to send an updated version of the Théâtre de la Mode on a tour of the United States, with the figurines dressed in the latest 1946 fashions. Jean Leguay, director of the "Art and Creation" Delegation in New York was the liaison between the Chambre Syndicale and the sponsoring group in New York: American Relief for France. He arranged to house the exhibition in the opulent Whitelaw Reid mansion at Madison Avenue and 50th Street. Georges Geffroy was put in charge of the interior design and several new sets were made in Paris to the specific layout of the mansion, among them one by the decorator Emilio Terry.

The team arrived in New York to help set up the exhibition well before the May 1 opening date. Madame Raymonde Scheikevitch remembers her role as that of Madame Broom, sweeping up after the workers, but when she walked down Fifth Avenue, many New Yorkers, recognizing that she was from Paris because of her chic clothes and her platform-soled shoes, waved and called out: "How's Paris?"[21]

The exhibition opened with a gala reception attended by the social and diplomatic elite of New York. Newspaper and magazine coverage was extensive, as it was both a social and an artistic event. As they went from décor to décor, New Yorkers commented: "Superb," "Marvelous." They were also dazzled by the tiny precious-stone or diamond jewelry such as Van Cleef's gem-studded épaulettes on a Schiaparelli evening dress or Cartier's "L'Oiseau en Cage" plastron for Worth. Twelve of the leading Paris jewelers had added their mite to the spectacle.

In New York, as in Paris, fashion was big business. During the war the American fashion industry had learned to do without inspiration and patterns from Paris. The Théâtre de la Mode helped reestablish French fashion leadership.

The wooden cases in which the dolls traveled across the Atlantic to present the new Spring-Summer 1946 fashions in the United States. This was the first collection for export since the Armistice in 1940.

At right: The poster for the Théâtre de la Mode exhibition in New York (May-June 1946), drawing by Christian Bérard.

continues on page 67

MAY-JUNE 1946

LE

THÉÂTRE
DE LA
MODE

EXHIBITION OF ART AND FASHION
CREATED BY FRENCH ARTISTS AND DESIGNERS
ORGANISED BY THE "CHAMBRE SYNDICALE DE LA COUTURE PARISIENNE"

PRESENTED BY "AMERICAN RELIEF FOR FRANCE"
AT THE BENEFICE OF ENTR'AIDE FRANÇAISE

451 MADISON AVENUE

DAILY : FROM 11 A.M. TO 10 P.M.
SUNDAY : FROM 12 A.M. TO 6 P.M.
ADMISSION 1 $ 20 (taxe included)

49

The Décors of Théâtre de la Mode

Set designers from Paris devoted their time and inspiration to create the *décors* for the original traveling Théâtre de la Mode exhibit in the late 1940s. Though the originals were lost, all but four were re-created for the second world tour in 1990.

This is the grand scale "Le Théâtre," (The Theater) originally created by Christian Bérard, above, and recreated by Anne Surgers (large photo). Shown at right is stage right box seating in the recreated décor.

In the photo on page 45 Bérard can be seen painting the décor.

"La Rue de la Paix en la Place Vendôme" originally created by Louis Touchagues (top far right) and re-created by Anne Surgers (below).

Near right is the original concept maquette for the décor.

More information about the designers of the décors on these pages can be found beginning on page 178.

André Beaurpair's "La Grotte Enchantée" (The Enchanted Grotto) original at far right,
and Anne Surgers' re-creation below.

Jean Cocteau's
"Ma Femme est
une Sorcière"
(My Wife is a
Witch), a tribute
to René Clair.
Original above,
Anne Surgers'
re-creation at
right.

Anne Surgers' re-creation
of André Dignimont's
"Palais Royal," at left.
The original is below and
the maquette below left.

The original "L'île de la Cité" by
Georges Douking, immediately above,
and Anne Surgers' re-creation, top.

Anne Surgers created "Scène
de Rue" ("Street Scene") as a
replacement for the Georges
Wakhevitch décor, "The Port of
Nowhere" (page 65).

The original "Croquis de Paris" (Paris Sketch) by Jean Saint-Martin, bottom, and Anne Surgers' re-creation, top.

Anne Surger's re-creation
of Jean-Denis Malclès
"Le Jardin Marveilleux"
(The Marvelous Garden),
above, and original at left.
Maquette below.

The Lost Décors

All of the original décors were lost after the Théâtre de la Mode completed its first world tour in San Francisco in 1946. The four on the following pages were not re-created for the second tour in 1990.

"Matin dans le Champs Elysées"
(Morning in the Champs Elysées)
by Emili Grau-Sala

"Le Port du Nulle Part" (The Port of Nowhere) by Georges Wakhevitch

"Un Salon de Style" (An At-Home) by Georges Geffroy

The original "Le Carrousel" (Merry-Go-Round)
décor, by Joan Rebull, has not been re-created.

continued from page 48

Women's Wear Daily covered the exhibition in depth. Fashion editors praised French taste and inventiveness. In the *Tobe Report* of May 2, 1946, fashion consultant Tobe wrote: "Words almost fail us in describing the beauty and exquisiteness of this exhibit. Certainly it is something that everyone in the retail and fashion business should see... It is one of the best educations in what fashion can mean that we know... Make no mistake about it – Paris is still the magic five-letter word." From New York the Théâtre de la Mode traveled to San Francisco, where the French community of 20,000 gave it an emotional and enthusiastic welcome. Sponsors in San Francisco included I. Magnin and two department stores owned by French families: the White House and the City of Paris. The exhibition opened on September 12, 1946, in the spacious galleries of the de Young Museum. Paul Caldaguès sent the following report to Paris:

> "The exhibition was inaugurated last night at 9:00 p.m. and was an enormous success. The atmosphere was even warmer, if possible, than in New York. All San Francisco society was there and remained at length in front of each one of the theatres...it had been a long time since an audience of such quality and quantity had been assembled (1,200 people)... The French Consul made a speech... the Mayor replied...he concluded, to great general emotion, by crying "Vive la France" three times. Then Madame Darius Milhaud read the letter from the Parisian seamstresses..."[22]

Mexico City, Chicago, and Dallas were among the many cities clamoring to host the exhibition after San Francisco, but none could offer the right package of a suitable site and sufficient funds to guarantee a surplus for L'Entraide Française. Once the exhibition closed at the de Young Museum, the dolls and the décors were stored at the City of Paris department store. By the early 1950s, the French couture houses were prospering again and, having served its purpose, the Théâtre de la Mode was abandoned by its French sponsors and presumed destroyed.

In September 1983, while doing research for a documentary on Dior at the de Young Museum, the curator of the textile department, Ana Bennett, told me about the Théâtre de la Mode. Naturally, I was most anxious to see these figurines dressed in the fashions of 1946 practically on the eve of Dior's New Look. The idea that the dolls had been presented in theater sets intrigued me and I was fascinated to hear that about 160 of them still existed and could be seen in vitrines at Maryhill, a small, eclectic museum perched on a bluff overlooking the Columbia River in Washington State.[23]

Several months later, as I was returning to Paris to continue my work on Dior, I decided to investigate the origins of the Théâtre de la Mode at the same time. I was fortunate enough to meet the son of Paul Caldaguès, Louis, who had kept a catalogue of the exhibition of 1945. In the spring of 1984 I met Boris Kochno and Henri Sauguet.

At the end of August of that year, during a stopover in the Portland, Oregon, airport, I was able to meet Linda Brady Tesner, who had just been named director of the Maryhill Museum. We discussed the possibility of organizing an exhibition of the figurines at the

For New York in 1946 a number of models wore real jewelry by leading Parisian jewelers. Diamonds and gold by Fontana for Molyneux (top photo); diamonds, rubies and platinum by Van Cleef & Arpels for Schiaparelli (bottom photo), the 1990 reproduction of which can be seen in color on page 174.

Museum of Kent State University where I teach. The new curator Stella Blum was one of the most eminent costume historians in the United States.

In November I went with Stella Blum to Maryhill. The figurines were even more extraordinary than we had imagined. They had not suffered greatly during their years of oblivion and seemed so many sleeping beauties waiting to be awakened.

In Paris, some weeks later, I discovered Jean Saint-Martin and Eliane Bonabel in their studio on the Rue de l'Odéon. Convinced for some forty years that the figurines had been destroyed, they were surprised and delighted to discover that such was not the case. In May 1985 I told the trustees of Maryhill about my research, concluding that one day the dolls should be sent back to Paris, restored, and shown there once again.

The death of Stella Blum put an end to the project of an exhibition of Théâtre de la Mode at Kent. I then decided to tell the whole story to Susan Train, Bureau Chief of Condé Nast Publications Inc. in Paris. She had heard of the Théâtre de la Mode when she had first come to Paris and her reaction was exactly what I had hoped: the figurines must return to Paris, be restored, and be exhibited at the new fashion museum then in construction.

Thus was born the Franco-American cooperation that was to result in the restoration and exhibition of the Théâtre de la Mode, still a symbol of the continuity of French creativity and of its cultural and artistic traditions. The aphorism "God is in the details" is attributed to Mies van der Rohe. It has never been more true than for the Théâtre de la Mode. And nothing could better express what it represents even today than the editorial published the day after the opening in New York in the *New York Herald Tribune* of May 2, 1946: "It is typical of the French spirit that artists, sculptors, and stage designers have collaborated with the houses of haute couture to create this magic. Whether one turns to the opera, to the street fair, to the night scenes, to the familiar streets, there is the same dignity, the same grace, the same poetry, telling the heroism of a city that in spite of terror and suffering saved itself whole, preserving alike its good taste, its loyalty to beauty, and its indefatigable skills."

*New York, Spring 1946. Eliane Bonabel showing a doll dressed by Balmain
to Carmel Snow and Diana Vreeland, editor-in-chief and fashion editor,
respectively, of* Harper's Bazaar.

The interviews concerning the Théâtre de la Mode were conducted by Stanley Garfinkel, professor of history at Kent State University. The tapes and the transcriptions of these interviews are kept in the oral history archives of the university. The transcriptions have been done by the Department of Applied Linguistics.

1. André Beaurepaire interview (May 27, 1988).
2. The Chambre Syndicale de la Couture Parisienne is a professional association created in 1868 to represent and defend the interests of the Paris couture houses.
3. Robert Ricci interview (June 6, 1988).
4. Eliane Bonabel interview (May 27, 1988).
5. Ibid.
6. Robert Ricci.
7. Madame Carven interview (December 22, 1988).
8. Eliane Bonabel.
9. Madame Martin (Claude Saint-Cyr), interview (January 10, 1989).
10. Jacques Mendel interview (January 9, 1989).
11. Eliane Bonabel.
12. Ibid.
13. Jean-Denis Malclès interview (May 27, 1989).
14. André Beaurepaire.
15. Jean-Denis Malclès.
16. Robert Ricci.
17. The French edition of *Vogue* ceased publication during the Occupation.
18. In French francs of 1945.
19. Robert Ricci.
20. Copy of a letter from Raoul Dautry, minister of reconstruction, to Ambassador René Massigli in the archives of the Théâtre de la Mode (Chambre Syndicale de la Couture).
21. Madame Raymonde Scheikevitch interview (June 6, 1989).
22. Report by Paul Caldaguès, Délégué Général, to the Chambre Syndicale de la Couture, September 1946 in the archives of the Chambre Syndicale de la Couture.
23. The 1946 dolls of the Théâtre de la Mode were saved by Paul Verdier, president of the City of Paris department store in San Francisco. Susan Train found, in the archives of the Chambre Syndicale de la Couture, the minutes of a meeting of the executive committee dated September 14, 1951, in which figure these lines: "The dolls in the storerooms of Mr. Verdier. Mr. Verdier once again insists to Mr. Barbas that the dolls of the Théâtre de la Mode should not be destroyed. He proposes, at his own expense, to send them to the Maryhill Museum. The executive committee agrees."

At right: An evening dress by Pierre Balmain in the Christian Bérard décor (New York, 1946)

*Hat by Albouy
(New York, 1946)*

*One of the trends for Spring-Summer 1946:
long hobble skirt, platter hat with egret feathers
reminiscent of pre-World War I fashions
(New York, 1946, Balmain model).*

In the Bérard "Le Théâtre," two Worth dresses with original jewelry by Cartier. On the right is the famous "Bird in a Cage," a plastron of diamonds, rubies, emerald, and sapphires. Reproductions may be seen in color on pages 174-175.

In New York, two models from the Spring-Summer 1946 collections: Hermès (left), Balmain (right). French fashion creativity is in full swing and wartime silhouettes are on the wane. New trends: shoulders are rounder, waists are emphasized, skirts are longer.

Haute Couture and Fashion 1939-1946

Nadine Gasc

"I tell myself I must save this diary to be reopened again at a later date when it will bear witness that in February 1941, between standing in line for milk, rutabagas, and mayonnaise with no oil or eggs, Candlemas with no crepes, and shoes with no leather, Paris brought forth its most characteristic feats, producing a *figured velvet dress...a very dressy pink lamé blouse...*" (Colette, Paris de ma fenêtre). That was how Colette described the Paris of 1941, where life was made up of daily hardship, of nostalgia for a suddenly vanished age, and the odd miracle of creativity.

The need to survive affected every aspect of daily existence in those days, and that went for the haute couture as well; the question of prestige took a backseat to the overriding need to protect the very existence of a profession, which at that time provided a million people with a livelihood, and to safeguard its capacity to create.

Women turning the pages of the rare fashion magazine published in those days may have had their secret dreams at the sight of the great couturiers' creations, but what they looked for in particular was the clever idea that would enable them to keep looking smart, or *coquette* as the term went then, an adjective that is no longer in use today but which for a long time was the very definition of a certain type of Parisienne, the sort that never ceased to taunt the Germans with their open display of ingenuity despite the fact that there was virtually nothing to be had.

Everything was strictly rationed. In June 1941 a "clothing" card was issued that was so complex that the *Petit Echo de la Mode* published a practical guide to enlighten its readers. Each card was worth a hundred points; a pittance, when one considers that a jacket containing a modest percentage of wool was worth forty points. Many women turned to little dressmakers for their wardrobe, but textiles too were strictly rationed: 4 yards 12 inches of fabric in 55-inch width were allowed for a coat; 1 yard 15 inches in 39-inch width for a shirt. The rules specifically stated, however, that exceptions could be made for "unusually tall people and pregnant women." One could also barter two old garments made of wool for a single new one, but this turned out to be a difficult operation as one had to refer to a table listing the only repairs that were allowed, in which the definition of old and new was more than arbitrary. As there was a rule against exchanging men's clothes for women's, the newspapers of the period carried patterns with which to transform a man's three-piece suit into a woman's suit.

How did the Parisienne fare in her struggle against deprivation, gloom, and hardship? We see her on her way through the streets of Paris on her bicycle, sporting a tailored suit with slightly outsized shoulders; a short skirt, naturally, for fabrics were scarce; her legs painted; platform shoes; the shoulder bag carefully not worn the same way as the

mailman's; and hats so fanciful and extravagant they bordered on the irreverent. Much prose had been devoted to those hats. On May 2, 1942, Jean Cocteau wrote in his diary that the hats worn by the "Effrayantes" reminded him of puff pastries made of tulle or of *perched berlingots* (twisted candies). Colette, too, wondered: "Is it out of gratitude for the savarin (sponge cake) we used to know that women now put *babas* on their heads?" In his memoirs, Christian Dior also mentioned those incredible hats: "Made of scraps that could not be used for anything else, they looked like huge pouffes that defied both the period's woes and plain common sense."

Such sartorial insouciance came as a shock to the women serving in the English and American armies who came to liberate Paris, yet it had served as a weapon against the austerity inflicted by the Germans, who had become so impatient with the general display of insolence that by 1944 they had threatened to close down every single milliner's shop. These quarrels between the Germans and the milliner's Chambre Syndicale were mere skirmishes, however, compared to the constant battle it took to keep the haute couture in Paris and to safeguard professional training. Lucien Lelong, who had been President of the Chambre Syndicale de la Couture since 1937 and became head of Group I of the Comité Général de l'Organisation de l'Industrie du Textile in 1942,[1] wrote a report on this struggle. It all began in late July 1940, when five German officers descended upon the Chambre Syndicale de la Couture's Paris headquarters, where they were greeted by Daniel Gorin, its secretary general. They left feeling rather dissatisfied with the evasive answers they had been given to their questions on the haute couture's current situation. A few days later they resorted to more expeditious methods, broke down the door, and impounded all of the archives, an important haul comprising documents on design, exports, and trade schools, plus the files on foreign buyers.

The German Reich planned to turn French haute couture into an official body with head offices in Berlin and Vienna. Faced with such a project, Lucien Lelong tried a number of arguments: "You can impose anything upon us by force, but Paris couture cannot be uprooted, neither as a whole nor in part. Either it stays in Paris or it does not exist. It is not within the power of any nation to steal fashion creativity, for not only does it function quite spontaneously, but also it is the product of a tradition maintained by a large body of skilled men and women in a variety of crafts and trades."[2]

When Lucien Lelong alerted the minister for production and labor of the serious danger facing the haute couture and its skilled labor, the Délégation Economique and the Chambre Syndicale asked him to go to Berlin "to try and save a French industry whose ruin would be beyond remedy and put the future of our economy in serious jeopardy." Keeping that industry and its skilled workers alive meant that, by the end of the war, "France would be in a position to earn substantial amounts of foreign currency in

The couturier Lucien Lelong was president of the Chambre Syndicale de la Couture from 1937 to 1945.

exchange for a minimum of raw materials and transportation, a great deal of inventiveness, and plain hard work. The figures show that before the war, export of a single dress made by a leading couturier enabled us to buy ten tons of coal; a liter of perfume was worth two tons of petrol; a bottle of champagne, three kilos of copper."[73]

Hats were the most important accessory because they gave a new look to an old outfit.

Above:
Madame Carven and visitors to the Théâtre de la Mode in Paris

On November 3, 1940, Lucien Lelong set out for Berlin with Daniel Gorin. Once there, he discovered that the Germans were setting up a fashion industry heavily subsidized by the government, the textile industry, and ready-to-wear manufacturers. Arguing that it was up to German fashions to stand on their own without relying on Paris, he claimed "for each country the right to create its own fashions." He refused the labor exchanges the Germans wanted from him; when they demanded that high-level French personnel be sent to found a school for advanced fashion skills, he stalled and asked for time to think it over. Upon his return to Paris, he had obtained the restitution of the archives.

Lucien Lelong's journey seemed to have accomplished something essential: French fashion was to remain in Paris and to keep its independence. That still left the problem of the textile shortages; after calculating the minimum quantities of fabric necessary for haute couture houses to continue to show seasonal collections of seventy-five models each, Lucien Lelong obtained from the official in charge of textiles at the Bureau for the Allocation of Industrial Products a system of rules for dispensation. Every house operating under this system was given a monthly allowance of 60 percent of the amount of fabric used during the same month in the year 1938. Later on, these allocations were based on the figures for actual consumption in 1942 and 1943.

These dispensations saved French couture from asphyxia, yet they merely added up to a reprieve that depended entirely on German tolerance and were in fact called into question on no less than fourteen occasions in less than four years' time, while at the same time a number of decrees were handed down in an attempt to interfere with the dynamism of French couture. Both exports and profits were forbidden, and press coverage was virtually nil because there were hardly any newspapers and magazines.

A mannequin (model) in a hat of fur and flowers by Gabrielle (1945)

Customers of the haute couture houses, however, were able to continue buying, thanks to the issue of *couture création*[4] cards, to be obtained in exchange for a substantial part of their clothing ration card.[5]

The Spanish couturier, Cristobal Balenciaga, who opened his Paris house in 1937

The system of dispensation went into effect in February 1941. The German authorities, who felt that no more than ten or twelve houses should qualify, asked to see a list of possible beneficiaries within forty-eight hours.

An initial selection of thirty-nine houses was accepted, but little by little the list grew until, by June 15, 1941, there were eighty-five of them. A month later Lucien Lelong, in order to have the privilege extended to houses of lesser importance, asked a commission of jurors made up of noncommercial professional experts such as teachers and artists to draw up a definitive list on the basis of models shown anonymously. The commission met three times and, despite German pressure, stood its ground in setting the number of selections at sixty.

On several occasions, however, Germans demanded more stringent limits on fabric allowances and tried to bring them down to the meager quantities allocated for the German ready-to-wear industry. In January 1944, as an example, they went so far as to close two leading Paris fashion houses, Grès and Balenciaga, on the grounds that they had gone beyond their rightful quantities of fabric. The house of Balenciaga only reopened thanks to the intervention of the Spanish Embassy, whereas Madame Grès had to put an end to the production of her draped designs. The profession as a whole shouldered responsibility for the salaries of her skilled workers during the time that the house remained closed, for it was felt that the German attack on the house of Grès was an attack on all of them. Becoming more demanding still, the Germans threatened to close down the haute couture once and for all in late July 1944. It was only saved from total extinction in extremis by the Liberation. Throughout its four-year struggle it had succeeded in maintaining its creativity and independence and had kept its skilled workforce, which meant that once again it was in a position to take its place in the overall French economy. The silk manufacturers had kept up production by turning their know-how to finding substitutes for the raw materials they needed; nylon thread having been allocated exclusively to the army's needs, rayon and synthetic fibers had now come to the fore.

The immediate postwar period was one of rebirth and prints were in again, in the form of motifs taken from Renaissance velvets,

Jacques Fath with one of his models for
the Théâtre de la Mode (1945)

Top: Rayond Barbas, president of the house of Patou

Bottom: A few days before the inauguration of the Théâtre de la Mode, Madame Lanvin takes a last look at one of her models.

Chinese vases, and Delft earthenware. Crepe, whether plain or printed, continued to carry the day in view of its fluidity and body, which it owed to the fact that its threads were twisted in the weaving. Plaids, polka dots, checks, and stripes (both nubby and contrasting matte and shiny) were still used as well. As for suits and coats, they came in herringbone and houndstooth fabrics and large checks. The house of Bucol had brought out a rainproof fabric known as *Contreplaqué* in 1944, which now became standard material for use in raincoats. As couturiers dressed their figurines for the Théâtre de la Mode in the spring of 1945, a new silhouette began to emerge. While shoulders were still important, they now owed their effect to the cut alone and were often accentuated by a pointed yoke inset that made waists look smaller. It was known as the V-line, for Victory.

Draped designs were back as well. They either emphasized plunging necklines (Pierre Balmain) or hips, formed an apron in front, or were gathered in the back in a sort of pouf (Balanciaga). Suit jackets softened, basques appeared that stood slightly away from the body, and pockets gained in size. For summer dresses, gathered skirts survived but now the fabric was gathered on the sides or in the back, instead of all around. Women continued to favor the three-quarter jackets called *canadiennes* that Marcel Rochas had introduced in the middle of the war, with their set-in belt and wide sleeves gathered at the wrist. Dressy clothes were short and trimmed with jet embroidery or braid. Evening dresses were still rare, due no doubt to the lack of gasoline, which made it difficult for people to get around. In her report on the 1945-1946 fall and winter collections, a journalist gave her article the title "Hésitation." Should one choose the wide or the narrow shape with its draped effect on the hips? Whatever one's preference, certain details were *de regueur* for those who wanted to be up-to-date: skirts had come down – hems were longer, now 17 inches from the ground – and buttons tended to be placed asymmetrically. For evening, necklines plummeted in the style of daring Eighteenth-century ones. Jacques Fath, for one, turned to Watteau and Fragonard for inspiration, and his models proudly paraded their 20-inch waistlines.

All of these trends were included in the spring-summer collections of 1946, the first to be designed for export since the war; the dresses worn by the figurines in the Théâtre de la Mode exhibition in New York give us a complete record of the event. These figurines wore small-scale replicas of the season's designs and were an excellent form of propaganda for French couture abroad. It is worth comparing them, in fact, to the ones shown in the fashion journals of the period.

Women, for all their hesitation before replacing the "parasol" shape with the "pen" silhouette, were still obliged to rethink their wardrobe. For one thing, fabrics and colors had all changed. The new woolens came in pastel shades; the silks now came in brocades and prints in bright colors. Rayon and crepe continued to hold sway. Another revolutionary development was the introduction of corsets. Marcel Rochas used belts to strangle the waist, Robert Piguet's waistcinch (called a *guêpière*) made hips look rounder, while Jacques Fath used strapless bras to show off a generous bosom. Skirts became longer still. Elegance was now a question of centimeters: hems must be at least nine centimeters (3.5 inches) below the knee. Stockings were once again an integral part of any given outfit.

For daytime the classic tailored suit was still in vogue (O'Rossen, 33), but it now had a rival in the form of a simple straight dress worn with a loose jacket of a different color (Robert Piguet, 83; Nina Ricci, 76).

The numbers in parentheses correspond to those used in the "Catalogue Raisonné" beginning on page 129, where there are color photographs of all mannequins.

(33)

(76)

Jacques Fath produced a design called "Poudre d'Iris" (15) – an easy jacket of beige wool that bloused slightly in the back and narrowed at the hips, with a straight black skirt to mid-calf – a typical example of the "pen-shaped" silhouette of flawless proportions. Meanwhile, Pierre Balmain broke new ground with a navy suit whose jacket flared away to show off a vest of white piqué (45). Journalists all approved of his gray and white wool coatdress that wrapped the body and buttoned asymmetrically (6).

(6)

Poudre d'Iris (15)

84

Draped fabrics hugging the body were everywhere in this collection; they were used by Jean Dessès (50), Nina Ricci (120), and Marcel Rochas (82). Paquin's Antonio del Castillo emphasized the hips of a black crepe dress with pleats of faille falling down the back (78). As for Balenciaga, the severity of his design is softened by a wide, draped sash ending in a fringe (5).

(5)

(82)

For summer, there was a play of stripes used in opposition to each other, as in *Sucre d'Orge* by Carven (48), Marcel Rochas (38), and Jacques Heim's dress with the shawl collar (59), as well as the similar work in the designs for evening by Mad Carpentier (174) and Agnès Drecoll (107).

(59)

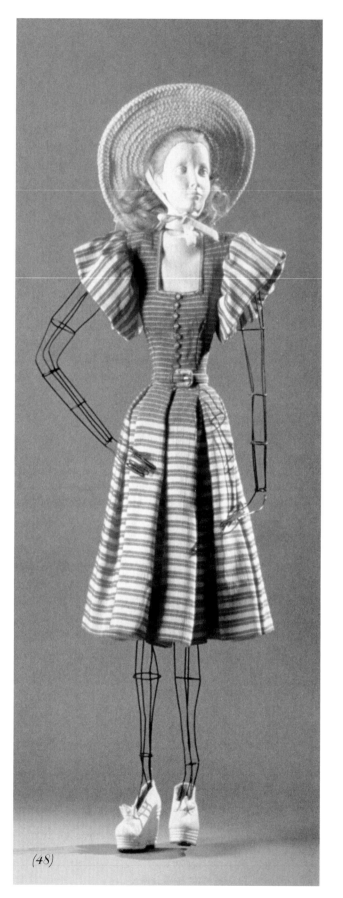

(48)

(174)

(107)

(38)

Two of Lucien Lelong's designs signaled a new trend. Christian Dior had entered the firm in 1941 and remained there till December 1946. There can be little doubt that he was responsible for the turquoise chiffon dress with white polka dots, for its low neckline with wide organdy collar bears the same stamp as certain creations of his shown in his first collection, that of Spring-Summer 1947; the only difference was in the length. A hint of the New Look to come also lay in the pink crepe party dress with the narrow bodice and fichu neckline that formed a contrast with the full skirt of black surah (117). Women took to dressing up more and more, either to go out or for parties given at home. Long, strapless evening dresses, which Jeanne Lanvin and Robert Piguet had designed as early as 1939, were back again. In his memoirs, Christian Dior wrote about the time he had spent working for the Piguet: "I think that at the time of the second collection I was able to make a truly personal contribution to the overall silhouette, namely the first full-skirted dresses." He continued along those lines, and two of those dresses, a white one and a black one, were photographed by Willy Maywald on the stairs inside the house of Robert Piguet (Paris *Couture-Années 30*, p. 45). In Lucien Lelong's "Faïence" (145) we find the same trend: ivory tulle embroidered with sequins in a gray-blue floral pattern. As the new ambassador for French couture, Michèle Morgan took it to America on her first trip there after the war.

The return of luxury after the austerity of war: black and silver brocade evening coat by Mad Carpentier (New York, 1946), next page.

(117)

(145)

The March 2, 1946, issue of *Elle* magazine shows Michèle Morgan and Danielle Darrieux attending the Paquin fashion show, both marveling at a violet satin evening gown draped at the hip in pink silk (154). In the same vein are the designs by Patou (182), Worth (189), Jeanne Lafaurie (142), and Marcel Rochas, whose layered flounces consisted of black tulle petals (185). Balenciaga weighed in with a high-necked, fitted bodice and wide, red satin skirt completely covered with ruby beading (161). Schiaparelli combined bands of different colored satin with silver lamé in a zigzag pattern (187).

(185)

(182)

(189)

An opposite trend consisted of long, buttoned sheaths and wide-brimmed hats with egrets, similar to the ones worn before World War I. Examples are Jacques Fath's black velvet *Caran d'Ache* (166) and the Balmain creation in which the draped skirt is held by a long cord (111). Robert Piguet featured a sheath with a long slit to make it easier to walk. The same silhouette turned up in the work of Germaine Lecomte (116), Lucien Lelong (173), and Jean Patou (155); these last two couturiers contrasted orange or pink crepe skirts with black bodices.

(166)

(111)

(116)

Two outstanding models from the 1946 collections drawn by René Gruau for French magazines, and shown in miniaturized version on the dolls of the Théâtre de la Mode. Above, by Jacques Fath. Next page, by Pierre Balmain.

Once the curtain came down on the Théâtre de la Mode, the play went on. The fashions of the 1940s had been left behind, and it was not until Yves Saint-Laurent's 1971 spring-summer collection that anyone ever thought of them again. In 1946, however, new trends and memories of fashions of the past converged in a veritable kaleidoscope, and creativity was once again unshackled.

Women everywhere bowed to the new image. They adopted tight, slit skirts that grew steadily longer, and learned to walk on stiletto heels once more. The shoulder bag made way for the purse or clutch bag. Waist cinches became a must for evening, to show off bust and bared shoulders. Holidays were in again, and women flocked to beaches for a tan. Starry-eyed, they followed these post-war fashions that culminated in the New Look (Spring-Summer 1947). The American press was the first to react. Having been cut off from French influence, American fashions had tried to create a style of their own. Seventh Avenue had taken off on its own. The New Look meant that once again the battle was on about the dictatorship of Parisian haute couture, and American women gave vent to their resistance by demonstrating in the streets.

French women also had their reservations about the upheaval. In its September 30, 1947, issue the magazine *Marie-France* published a referendum "for or against long skirts." The way it framed its questions was most interesting: "Every one of you is wondering: Why? What will be the consequences? How can we adapt?" The lines that followed were both ironic and to the point: "Everyone has an opinion on the subject, yet everyone feels powerless when it comes to anything as mysterious as fashion." That, in a nutshell, perhaps summed it all up.

Translated by Nina de Voogd from the original 1989 French essay

EDITOR'S NOTES

1. This report was presented to the Chambre Syndicale de la Couture, November 8, 1944.
2. Ibid.
3. Ibid.
4. According to the Lelong report, "The number of couture-création cards delivered to French clients between August 20, 1941, and December 31, 1943, was 19,015; the number of cards delivered to the authorities of the Hotel Majestic who reserved the right to deliver them to non-French citizens was 200. These cards were never renewed."
5. The couture houses were also made responsible for collecting used clothing for the Secours National. Lucien Lelong, as president, imposed a 5 percent tax on all couture sales again to benefit the Secours National, which by June 30, 1944, totalled close to 55 million francs.

Christian Dior on the eve of his first collection in February 1947. His famous "New Look" (right) closed once and for all the era of wartime fashions.

The Rehearsal

David Seidner

When Susan Train asked me to do the photographs of the Théâtre de la Mode, my first reaction was enthusiastic. It was only later, when considering the idea of spending one month with dolls dressed from head to toe in fashions of 1946, that I began to have doubts. In the past I had done still lifes of costumes on headless dress forms that left room for the viewer to dream, but here the task was more specific, therefore more difficult. My fear was realized from minute one. How was I to show the scale of the dolls? I tried everything imaginable. At the end of two weeks of incredible tension – just try to make wire dolls with plaster heads stand on their own in believable pose – I realized that these dolls were not really miniatures but a group of beings in their own right who did exactly as they pleased, and I stopped resisting. Some, of course, were charming and cooperative, others capricious. Some were sophisticated, others provincial. Some were so convincing that it was frightening to watch them come to life under the lights, and some were just impossible. Many times I wanted to throw in the towel. How to make them live? As in the theater, I rehearsed and shot each photo two or three times.

At night, when silence and isolation exaggerated the pathos and obstinacy of these phantoms, I would begin to swear at them and my assistant would sigh, "c'est l'heure." But little by little I fell under their spell and found it difficult to leave the studio each night. This magic theater. A strange kind of parentheses on an extended reality took place, and in my voyeurism the roles were reversed: I became the stubborn, implacable still life, while the little ladies looked on.

The numbers in parentheses on David Seidner's photographs on pages 97-128 correspond to those used in the "Catalogue Raisonné" at the back of the book.

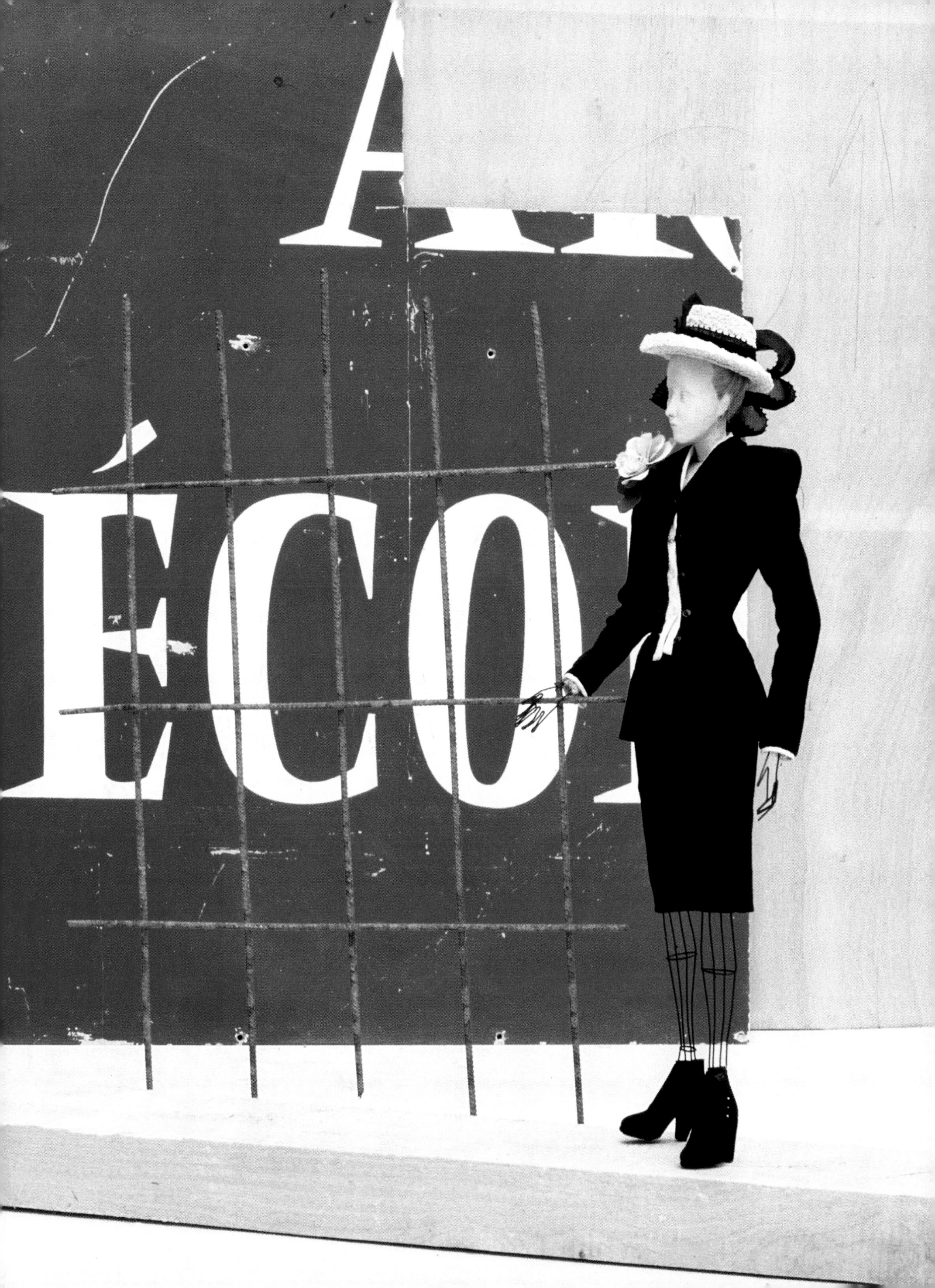
ÉCO

(186)

(94)

108

(82)

(72)

110

(39)
(51)

(10)

112

116

Catalogue Raisonné of the Models

This catalogue of the Thèâtre de la Mode mannequins was originally created by Nadine Gasc and Veronique Belloir for the 1990 tour, which began in Paris and included an exhibit at the Metropolitan Museum of Art in New York. Photographs are by Laurent Sully-Jaulmes. Translated from the French by Jacqueline Horscher Thomas.

The numerical order of this catalogue follows that of the Chambre Syndicale de la Couture established for the exhibition held in New York in May-June 1946. The original numbers have also been used for the list of missing models at the end of the catalogue. Roman numerals have been used for models that do not appear on the Chambre Syndicale list or when attribution has not been possible. The colors described are those of the original models, some of which are now faded.

1   *2*

1. Agnès Drecoll
Double-breasted day dress in greige wool crepe. Long sleeves, shawl collar, side-draped bodice continuing over the shoulders and held by a rounded yoke in back. Flared skirt with double inverted pleats.
Wide brim hat in rust felt with beige braid and cord trim ending in two pompons: **Gaby Mono.** Coiffure: **Prévost.**
Platform shoes in beige and brown suede: **Der-Balian.**
Buttons: **Richard.** Belt: **Germaine Paré.**
Décor: **André Dignimont.**

2. Alex
Coat and dress ensemble. Dress in black wool crepe with front buttoning. Loose raglan coat in large black-and-white diagonal wool plaid with green crepe facings and cuffs. Originally, the dress had white piqué collar and lapels.
White felt hat with black grosgrain ribbon trimmed with white flowers and veiling: **Maude & Nano.** Coiffure: **Georgius.**
Shoes (missing): **Daliet-Grand.**
Décor: **Jean Saint-Martin.**

3. Ana de Pombo
Day dress and jacket ensemble. Dress with pleated skirt in ivory crepe (synthetic), yellow patent leather belt. The yellow crepe (synthetic) jacket has rows of horizontal pleats extending over the three-quarter-length sleeves.
Picture hat in black (artificial) straw with black velvet ribbon and veil: **Albouy.** Coiffure: **Azéma.** Black suede wedge sandals trimmed in gold leather: **Grezy.**
Décor: **Louis Touchagues.**

3

4

5

6

8

9

10

4. Anny Blatt

Hand-knitted ensemble. Single-breasted, four-button red wool jacket with flat collar, patch pockets and narrow self-belt over gray wool pleated skirt with red stripes.
Béret (missing): **Anny Blatt.** Coiffure: **Luzic.**
Shoes (missing): **Greco.** Gray knit mittens with red leather appliqués: **Codet & Teilliet.**
Décor: unknown.

5. Balenciaga

Black wool suit. Four-button, single-breasted fitted jacket. Around the hips, a wide, black silk faille, knotted sash with silk fringe.
Natural-color straw hat trimmed with black ostrich feathers: **Balenciaga.** Coiffure: **Georgel.** Shoes (missing): **Vaginay.**
Décor: **André Dignimont.**
References: *Vogue*, Summer 1946, p. 108.
L'Officiel, April 1946, p. 79.

6. Pierre Balmain

Coatdress (originally belted) in gray and white heather wool, wrapped and buttoned asymmetrically with silver ball buttons. Side trim, bow, and cuffs in white silk.
White (artificial) straw hat with matching feathers: **Maud Roser.** Coiffure: **Guillaume.** Platform, ankle-strap sandals in white leather: **Casale.** Black umbrella: **Vedrennes.** Gloves (missing): **Faré.**
Décor: **Louis Touchagues.**
References: *Plaire*, Album de Luxe, 1946, No. 3, p. 100.
Elle, April 9, 1946, p. 17.

8. Bruyère

Buttoned-through dress in blue linen. Cape collar and short sleeves with two ruffles trimmed in blue and white passementerie.
Matching blue linen hat with white bias band tied in the back (synthetic): **Bruyère.** Coiffure: **Luzic.** Blue linen sandals with white stitching: **Hellstern.** Mauve-and-white striped parasol: **Ladousse.**
Décor: **André Dignimont.**

9. Carven. "Après l'Ondée"

Belted trench coat in Bucol almond-green gabardine lined in green and white (synthetic) crepe print. Brown leather-trimmed belt with buckle.
Hat in matching stitched gabardine: **Simone Cange.** Coiffure: **Gabriel Fau.** Brown-leather wedge shoes with buckle: **Argence.**
Décor: **André Dignimont.**
References: *L'Art et la Mode*, January-February 1946, p. 49.
Plaire, Album de Luxe, 1946, No. 3, p. 197.
L'Officiel, April 1946, p. 79.

10. Marcelle Chaumont

Day dress in navy wool crepe closed on each side by four white buttons. V-necked top with M.C. embroidered initials. Extended shoulders over long, full sleeves in white (synthetic) crepe with elasticized wrists. Gathered skirt from long torso.
Fabric: **Porter, Bennet & Gaucheranol.** Large white straw hat with navy and white feathers: **Le Monnier.** Coiffure: **Lebreuilly.** Shoes (missing): **Bunting.** Buttons: **Desrues.**
Décor: **André Dignimont.**
Reference: *La Femme Chic*, 1946, Special Collection issue, p. 42.

11. Marcel Dhorme

Sports ensemble. Three-button long, fitted jacket in green gabardine with fake bolero top and four flap pockets. Greige gabardine straight skirt with front pleat. Originally, a greige and white dotted scarf was tied around the neck.
Matching green turban with tassel: **Simone Cange.** Coiffure: **Marcel Birot.** Sling-back platform sandals in charcoal gray suede: **Léandre.** Brown leather shoulder bag with white saddle-stitching: **Mabille.**
Décor: **André Dignimont.**

12. Marcelle Dormoy

Day ensemble. Three-quarter dolman-sleeved top in ochre, green, and rust horizontal-striped linen (synthetic) with three buttons. The skirt in solid rust linen, closed on both sides by three buttons, conceals shorts.
Coiffure: **Arvet Thouvet.** Wedge sandals, white wooden soles with twisted striped linen top.
Décor: **André Dignimont.**

14. Dupouy-Magnin

Sport suit in burgundy-and-white tweed (wool blend). Long fitted jacket with shawl collar, red leather belt. Two large pouch pockets with side openings trimmed with burgundy leather tabs also repeated at the shoulder yoke. Gored tweed skirt. White satin crepe shirt with stitched pointed collar.
Red felt hat with fringed jersey band tied in back: **Jane Blanchot.** Coiffure: **Elysées-Coiffure.** Burgundy leather oxfords with white leather stitching: **Gelé.** Burgundy leather agenda: **Arcelle.**
Décor: **Georges Douking.**

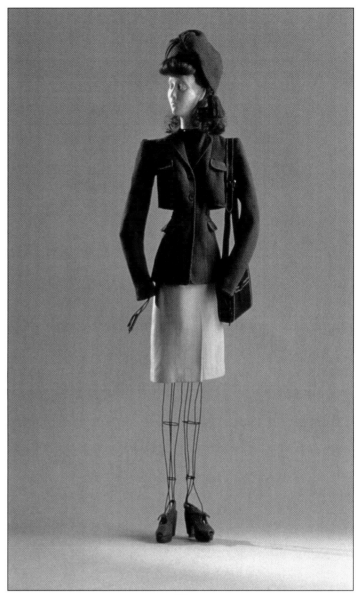

11

8

12

14

15   *16*

17   *18*

19   *21*

15. Jacques Fath. "Poudre d'Iris"

Ensemble. Three-quarter-length jacket in sand wool narrowing to hem with unpressed pleats from the shoulders. Peter Pan collar, low three-black-button closing. Narrow black wool skirt. This design was part of the *ligne stylo* ("pen line") collection launched by Jacques Fath for Spring 1946.
Small black (artificial) straw hat with black velvet ribbon and egret feathers: **Jacques Fath.** Coiffure: **Gervais.** Shoes (missing): **Jordan.** Black suede gloves: **Codet & Teilliet.** Bag (missing): **Mabille.**
Décor: **Georges Wakhevitch.**
References: *L'Art et la Mode*, Spring-Summer 1946, p. 19.
La Femme Chic, Spring-Summer 1946, p. 49.

16. Gaston

Red wool dress with three self-covered buttons. Dropped shoulders. Short puffed sleeves trimmed in scalloped écru linen. The fitted bodice is accentuated by stitched edge-to-edge tucks. Gored skirt. Wool and linen belt. Originally, the dress had a collar matching the sleeve trim.
Picture hat in berry-red straw with white piping and bow trim: **Maud Roser.** Coiffure: **Henri Durand.** Red and white flat shoes with small platforms and tasseled lacings: **Costa.**
Décor: **André Dignimont.**

17. Jacques Heim

Beachwear ensemble. Paréo pants, bra, and split skirt in printed linen (Riqueur) with giant red and green stylized flowers. Wide-brimmed natural straw hat with black velvet ribbon and cherries: **Jacques Heim.** Coiffure: **Jacques Cohen.** Red and white crisscross leather platform sandals: **Hellstern.**
Décor: **Joan Rebull.**
Reference: *Elle*, July 23, 1946, p. 12.

18. Henry à la Pensée

Day ensemble. Gray wool dress with shirt collar and gray-and-mauve striped wool tie. Slim skirt with crossed drape over the hips. Loose jacket to match with mauve facings.
Lilac suede toque with self fringe: **Jane Blanchot.** Coiffure: **Desfossés.** Shoes (missing): **Grezy.** Lilac suede gloves: **Henry à la Pensée.**
Décor: **Georges Douking.**

19. Hermès

Sportswear ensemble. Two-button honey suede jacket with slit pockets, notched collar, raglan sleeves, and gold-buckled belt. Black saddle-stitching.
Straight skirt in black wool crepe.
Coiffure: **Antoine.** Honey suede oxfords with black stitching and black platform soles: **Hellstern.** Black suede gloves with yellow seams: **Hermès.**
Décor: **André Dignimont.**

20. Jeanne Lafaurie

Square-necked draped dress in sulfur yellow (synthetic) jersey with short sleeves and back buttoning. The finely pleated asymmetric draping of the top extends into the full skirt. Purple suede belt with arrow pierced heart-shaped buckle. Purple suede brimmed hat edged in parma grosgrain ribbon: **Maude & Nano.** Purple suede platform sandals wrapped around the ankle: **Casale.** Small purple suede purse: **Mabille.** Purple suede gloves: **Dumont.**
Décor: **Louis Touchagues.**

21. Jeanne Lanvin

Day dress in pale pink linen with notched collar, three-quarter-length sleeves, wrapover bodice with shoulder yoke, pointed front insert. Full gored skirt with matching belt trimmed in green felt with gold nailheads.
Pale green woven rough straw hat bordered in pink linen: **Jeanne Lanvin.** Coiffure: **Rambaud.** Shoes (missing): **Hellstern.** Handbag (missing): **Jeanne Lanvin.** Gloves (missing): **Faré.**
Décor: **André Dignimont.**

23. Lucien Lelong

Cap-sleeved dotted turquoise and white chiffon dress with cowl-draped bodice. White organdy collar and cuffs. Matching chiffon sash wrapped and tied in a large bow. Natural straw picture hat with ivory grosgrain ribbon: **Legroux.** Coiffure: **Charbonnier.** Shoes (missing): **Elie.** Gloves (missing): **Faré.**
Décor: **André Dignimont.**
References: *Vogue*, Summer 1946, p. 156, photo Horst. *Claudine*, May 29, 1946, cover: photo Pottier. *Marie France*, June 19, 1946, p. 11.

24. Mad Carpentier

Day ensemble. Waist-length blouson in ochre and brown wool houndstooth check worked on the bias. Three buttons, small stand-up collar, wide raglan sleeves. A-line skirt in brown wool with patch pockets and deep front pleat concealing buttons.
Béret in matching houndstooth with feathers and veil: **Albouy.** Coiffure: **Jacqueline.** Flat brown suede shoes with fringed tongues: **Maniatis.** Brown suede gloves.
Décor: **Georges Douking.**

20

19

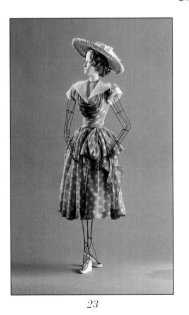

23

24

25   *27*

25. Maggy Rouff

Beachwear ensemble in off-white cotton toile. Short buttoned bolero with puff sleeves, bare midriff, and long swing skirt worn over shorts. The patch pockets and hem are trimmed with brown, black, and green bias bands.
Bronze-green wide-brimmed woven straw hat: **Gilbert Orcel.**
Green shantung and beige suede platform sandals: **Casale.**
Accessories (missing): **Winter.**
Décor: **Joan Rebull.**

26. Lucile Manguin. "Barbizon"

Day ensemble. Long double-breasted fitted jacket in absinthe-and-black wool check. Notched collar. Basque cut on the bias. Collar and pockets trimmed in black passementerie. Pleated black wool skirt.
Small black straw hat with black velvet ribbon trim: **Lucille Manguin.** Coiffure: **Alex Tonio.** Black suede shoes. Black suede bag. Black umbrella with matching checked cover: **Vedrennes.**
Décor: **Louis Touchagues.**
Reference: *L'Officiel*, April 1946, p. 40.

27. Marcelle Alix

Day ensemble. Red wool dress and fur jacket. The dress has a V-shaped yoke in back that holds fan draping, becoming a capelet in front. Long, finely pleated sleeves. Straight skirt in front, stitched and released pleats from the yoke in back. Fur jacket lined in matching red wool with fold at shoulder, making extended-cap sleeves.
Wide wavy-brim red straw hat with grosgrain hatband: **Simone Cange.** Coiffure: **Roger Para.** Red leather laced platform shoes: **Daliet Grand.**
Décor: unknown.

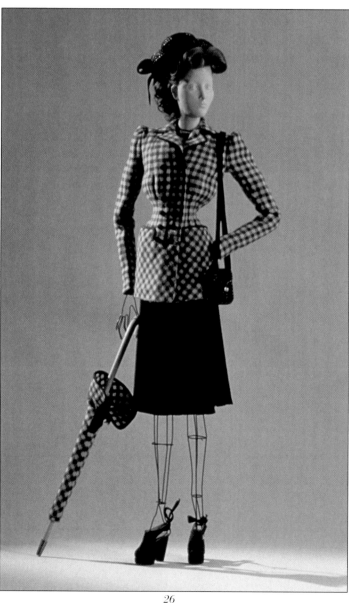

26

31

28. Martial & Armand

Day ensemble in yellow-and-brown houndstooth wool (Lesur).
Long fitted jacket with set-in sleeves and stand-up collar.
Horizontal bias bands at bust and hips trimmed with leather
and small gold chains. Brown leather belt. Skirt with deep,
rolled inverted pleat on one side.
Brown felt hat with feather: **Blanch & Simone.** Coiffure:
Villamor & Gille. Sling wedges with brown and beige leather
and suede top: **Bertili.** Belt and leather trim: **Lalo.**
Décor: **Georges Douking.**
Reference: *La Femme Chic*, 1946, Special Collection issue,
p. 64.

29. Mendel

Bright blue wool suit. Two-button single-breasted long jacket.
Shawl collar trimmed with white piqué and slotted buttoned
tabs. Raglan sleeves, sunburst tucks at the shoulders and on
the large pockets. Skirt with deep front pleat.
Large sailor hat in white (artificial) straw trimmed in white
flowers and blue grosgrain: **Nelly Levasseur.** Coiffure:
Desfossés. Ankle strap shoes in blue and white leather and
suede: **Casale.** White kid gloves tied with blue leather: Hermès.
Handbag (missing): **Choses d'Art.**
Décor: **Louis Touchagues.**

30. Molyneux

Day ensemble. Redingote in beige wool with small collar,
trimmed with passementerie cording, worn over soft skirt in
black satin crepe (synthetic).
Small black straw hat with grosgrain ribbon and veiling:
Molyneux. Coiffure: **Desfossés.** Black leather platform sling-
back shoes: **Gillet.** Black leather handbag (missing): **Model.**
Décor: **Jean Saint-Martin.**

31. Charles Montaigne

Day ensemble. Navy blue redingote with three gold initial M
buttons. Notched collar and basque effect trimmed in navy
and white passementerie. Slit pockets. Matching skirt has
deep front pleat.
Small white (artificial) straw hat trimmed with flowers: **Sygur.**
Coiffure: **Azema.** Navy blue leather wedge sandals: **Grezy.**
Buttons: **Desrues.** White kid gloves with navy stitching
and seaming.
Décor: **Louis Touchagues.**

33. O'Rossen

Day suit in brown-and-beige wool tweed with fine yellow and
blue stripes. Long one-button jacket, notched collar and flap
pockets. Straight skirt. Mustard satin crepe blouse (synthetic).
Ochre felt béret trimmed with feathers: **Rose Descat.** Coiffure:
AGG. Oxfords in brown leather and suede: **Greco.** Mustard
suede gloves: **Hermès.**
Décor: **Georges Douking.**

34. Paquin

Brown linen day dress with white organdy collar. Short raglan
sleeves and flared A-lined skirt. Bias bands of white linen on
sleeves and around torso from bust to hip.
Brown straw hat: **Paquin.** Coiffure: **Jean-Pierre.** Brown linen
sling-back platform sandals: **Richomme.** Gloves (missing):
Faré.
Décor: **Georges Douking.**
References: *Fémina*, May 1946, p. 143, drawing by Claire
Favée. *L'Art et la Mode*, Spring-Summer 1946, cover.

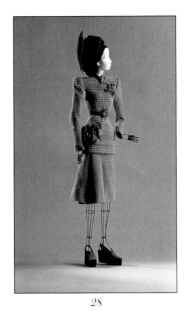

28   29

30   31

33   34

36

37

38

36. Raphaël

Long-sleeved day dress in black-and-white houndstooth wool belted in black leather. Fitted bodice with small collar. Paneled skirt with slanted pockets trimmed with the fabric selvage. Picture hat in black (artificial) straw, lined and trimmed in red linen and black braid: **Raphaël.** Coiffure: **Antonio.** Black leather wedge sling-back shoes: **Léandre.** Red leather bag: **Lalo.** White kid gloves.
Décor: **André Dignimont.**

37. Georgette Renal

Day dress with elbow-length cuffed sleeves in gray-blue and white heather wool. Stand-up collar closed by two leather buttons. Tucks from bust to hip released into inverted pleat panel. Straight skirt. Leather and fabric belt.
Ice blue and havana felt hat with turned-up brim held by feather: **Maude & Nano.** Coiffure: **Georgius.** Brown leather oxfords with cork soles: **Penthesilée.** Havana leather gloves: **Faré.**
Décor: **Georges Douking.**
Reference: *Fémina*, May 1946, p. 139.

38. Marcel Rochas

Slim dress in mauve-and-white striped broadcloth (synthetic) with tucked torso, short puff sleeves and white piqué collar and cuffs. Hip drape held on one side with violets falling over the straight skirt.
White (artificial) straw hat, white grosgrain hatband and veil: **Maude & Nano.** Coiffure: **Gervais.** Matching fabric platform sling sandals: **Léandre.** Flowers: **Judith Barbier.** Accessories (missing): **Suviane.**
Décor: **Louis Touchagues.**
References: *Elle*, June 4, 1946, p. 11. *Vogue*, Summer 1946, p. 157 and 138. *Album de la Mode du Figaro*, Summer 1946, p. 82. *Silhouette*, May 1946, p. 19.

43

39. Robert Piguet

Navy blue crepe day suit (synthetic). Four-button jacket slightly fitted in the front. Round collar trimmed with white piqué ruffle. white piqué cuffs. Flapped patch pockets. Straight skirt with side slit.
Hat in navy (artificial) straw and white piqué with veil: **Paulette.** Coiffure: **Antonio.** Stitched navy leather platform wedge sandals with ankle straps: **Argence.** White piqué gloves.
Décor: **Louis Touchagues.**
Reference: *Silhouette.* May 1946. p. 19.

40. Schiaparelli

Afternoon dress in yellow-and-black printed crepe with Place Vendôme pattern. High scarf neck and "chopped" kimono sleeves. Bolero effect. Bias skirt sashed at the waist by a self-belt tied in the back.
Small bowler in black straw with matching grosgrain tied in the back: **Schiaparelli.** Coiffure: **Marc Ruyer.** Long black suede gloves: **Faré.** Sandals in black linen and leather: **Casale.**
Décor: **André Dignimont.**

41. Véra Borea

Skirt and blouse ensemble. Back-buttoned red-and-white checked linen (synthetic) bias skirt on yoke with twisted suspenders. White linen blouse (synthetic) with notched collar, short sleeves, and three buttons.
Coiffure: **Simoneau.** Wedge sandals in white leather with ankle straps: **Codreanu.** Straw basket holding flowers and fruits: **Judith Barbier.** Buttons: **Desrues.**
Décor: **Joan Rebull.**
References: *Album de la Mode du Figaro.* Summer 1946, p. 73.
Jardin des Modes. Summer 1946. p. 34.
Plaire. Summer 1946. p. 51.

42. Worth

Day ensemble. Red wool double-breasted three-quarter-length box jacket. Notched collar, silver ball buttons. Four large slanted pockets with horizontal stitched-pleat details. Straight skirt in gray wool with red and white pinstripe. Blouse in ivory crepe (synthetic). Red patent leather belt.
Stitched ivory felt hat, white grosgrain, and bird of paradise feather: **Maud Roser.** Coiffure: **Gabriel Fau.** High heel ankle-strap platform shoes in white and red leather with open toes: **Casale.** White kid gloves with red wool cuffs: **Faré.**
Décor: **Jean Saint-Martin.**

43. Agnès Drecoll

Long-sleeved pale blue wool afternoon dress. Fitted bodice. draped V-neck held by two leaves of gathers with cord trim. Gathered skirt with deep front pleat.
Hat (missing): **Gaby Mono.** Coiffure: **Prévost.** Shoes (missing): **Der-Balian.**
Décor: **Louis Touchagues.**

44. Ana de Pombo

Cocktail dress with three-quarter-length sleeves and raised shoulders in pale pink satin crepe (synthetic). Armholes and hips trimmed with swags of fine pleats. Full gored skirt.
Hat (missing): **Albouy.** Coiffure: **Azema.** Navy stitched leather ankle-strap wedge sandals: **Grezy.**
Décor: **Georges Wakhevitch.**

39

40

41

42

43

44

45

46

47

48

49

50

45. Pierre Balmain

Day suit in navy blue wool. Fitted jacket over white piqué vest. Slit pockets. Pink rose on the shoulder. Straight skirt. Straw hat with large navy organdy cabbage rose in back: **Jeannette Colombier.** Coiffure: **Guillaume.** Black suede side-buttoned ankle boots: **Casale.** Umbrella (missing): **Vedrennes.** Gloves (missing): **Faré.** Flowers: **Judith Barbier.** Décor: **Louis Touchagues.**
References: *Album de la Mode du Figaro,* Summer 1946, p. 9, photo J. Moral. *Vogue,* Summer 1946, p. 161, drawing by A. Delfau. *Elle,* April 30, 1946, p. 11. *L'Officiel,* April 1946, p. 46.

46. Pierre Benoît

Cocktail dress in elephant-gray crepe (synthetic). Back-buttoned draped bodice with twisted knot in front extending over the hips. The waist is marked by green and white beaded trim. Straight skirt with pleated panels in back.
Black straw picture hat lined in black tulle: **Gilbert Orcel.** Coiffure: **Pourrière.** Sling-back black suede wedge sandals with crystal beading: **Inabilac.**
Décor: **Jean Saint-Martin.**

47. Bruyère

Cocktail dress. High-rising black wool skirt buttoned at waist. Back drape held by black satin bow. Ivory crepe top (synthetic) with silk tone-on-tone embroidery. Short sleeves with black wool cuffs.
White (artificial) straw boater trimmed in black lace: **Bruyère.** Coiffure: **Luzic.** Black suede sandals with white leather piping: **Georgette.** Black antelope suede and satin pouch held by tasseled passementerie cord: **Model.**
Décor: **Jean Saint-Martin.**

48. Carven. "Sucre d'Orge"

Pink-and-white horizontal candy-striped shantung daydress with deep square neck. The long buttoned bodice is finely tucked to conceal the white stripe. Short, full cap sleeves, self-belt, skirt with deep folds.
Natural straw hat with white grosgrain trim: **Jane Blanchot.** Coiffure: **Gabriel Fau.** White leather platform wedge shoes: **Argence.**
Décor: **André Dignimont.**
References: *Silhouette,* May 1946, p. 14 and p. 73. *Plaire,* Album de Luxe, 1946, No. 3, p. 311. *Elle,* July 30, 1946, p. 16. *Fémina,* May 1946, p. 101.

49. Marcelle Chaumont

Fitted coatdress in brick-red linen with four covered buttons, opening over a white (synthetic) crepe panel. A stitched flap extends over wide raglan sleeves. Buttonhole pockets piped in white crepe to match the false cuffs.
White straw toque trimmed with flowers: **Le Monnier.** Coiffure: **Lebreuilly.** Red leather ankle-strap platform shoes: **Bunting.** Buttons: **Desrues.**
Décor: **Louis Touchagues.**

50. Jean Desses

Dress and jacket ensemble. Fitted dress in black-and-white houndstooth twill (synthetic) with side front buttoning. Straight skirt with hip draping tied in the back and falling in a panel. Jacket in black (synthetic) crepe with lining, pockets, and cuffs to match the dress.
Hat (missing): **Rose Valois.** Coiffure: **Gervais.** Black suede wedge shoes with straps: **Drettas.** Accessories (missing): **Paulette.** Black suede gloves.
Décor: unknown.
Reference: *Vogue,* Summer 1946, p. 161.

51. Marcel Dhorme

Day suit in navy blue linen trimmed in white piqué. Double-breasted jacket with fake bolero effect. White piqué collar, cuffs, pocket tabs, and yoke. High-waisted skirt.
White straw boater with navy grosgrain ribbon and veil: **Simone Cange.** Coiffure: **Marcel Birot.** Navy platform sling shoes: **Léandre.** Handbag (missing): **Mabille**
Décor: **Louis Touchagues.**

52. Marcel Dormoy

Two-piece day ensemble in turquoise (synthetic) crepe. Bias tunic, three-quarter-length sleeves, trimmed at the neck with a bias of white piqué. Tucked detailing at the bust and hips. A-line skirt with deep back pleats.
Purple moiré hat with rolled brim, trimmed with roses and veil tied in the back: **Claude Saint-Cyr.** Coiffure: **Arvet Thouvet.** White leather platform wedge shoes with ankle straps: unknown.
Décor: **Louis Touchagues.**

53. Madeleine de Rauch

White linen ensemble (synthetic). Long fitted tunic with short sleeves, notched collar. V-neck to waist over modesty panel. Raised embroidery on basque. Rust suede leather belt. Straight skirt with deep back pleats.
Large boater in rust straw with veil and rust velvet ribbon: **Madeleine de Rauch.** Coiffure: **Marc Ruyer.** White suede pumps: **Daliet-Grand.** Long rust suede gloves: **Faré.** Belt: **Winter.** Handbag (missing): **Lalo.**
Décor: **Louis Touchagues.**
References: *Jardin des Modes, Plein Eté*, 1946, p. 38. *L'Officiel*, April 1946, p. 131.

51   *53*

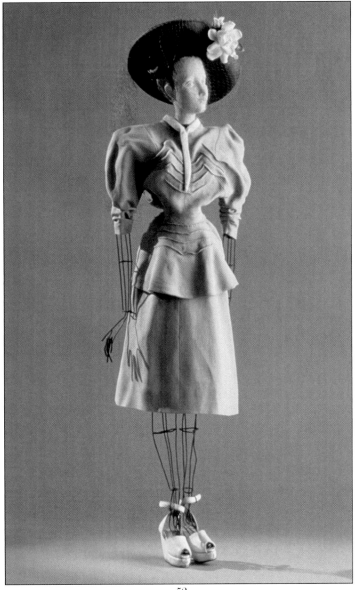

52

49

54

55

56

57

59

60

54. Dupouy-Magnin

Royal blue and white linen dress (synthetic). Sweetheart neckline, draped bodice. Large white scalloped collar trimmed in the back with an embroidered butterfly. The same butterfly trims the cuffs. Flared skirt of blue and white scalloped bands.
Hat (missing): **Jane Blanchot.** Coiffure: **Elysées-Coiffure.** Shoes (missing): **Gelé.** Embroideries: **Roger.**
Décor: unknown.

55. Jean Farell

Black (synthetic) crepe dress with three-quarter sleeves. Spiral draping tying in the back. Each shoulder is trimmed with an insert of gold sequin and pearl embroidery.
Hat (missing): **Albouy.** Coiffure: **Gervais.** Shoes (missing): **Thomas.**
Décor: **Jean-Denis Malclès (?).**
Reference: *L'Art et la Mode,* Spring-Summer 1946. p. 106.

56. Jacques Fath. "Longchamp Fleuri"

Gray wool suit lined in mauve linen (synthetic). Mauve linen blouse. Corselet skirt. Gray and pink silk embroidered flowers around neck and at hip.
Mauve straw picture hat trimmed with black velvet ribbon: **Jacques Fath.** Coiffure: **Gervais.** Black suede open-toed, high-heeled sling shoes: **Jordan.** Small gray suede drawstring purse: **Mabille.** Pearl gray suede gloves with matching embroidery. Gold-plated chain necklace: **Desrues.**
Décor: **Louis Touchagues.**

57. Gabrielle. "Paris"

Afternoon ensemble. Pistachio wool coat closed by self-belt with horseshoe buckle. Stitched detailing at shoulders. Released tucks from waist in back. Black crepe dress with pistachio necktie and front panel under split skirt.
Black and pistachio hat with feathers: **Gabrielle.** Coiffure: **Antoine.** Black suede wedge sandals: **Crézy.** Belt: **Mabille.** Black crepe gloves.
Décor: **Georges Douking.**

58. Gaston

Pale pink crepe dress (synthetic). Long buttoned sleeves. draped top with beaded corselet in iridescent pearls and sequins. Easy skirt with front gathers.
Large black felt hat lined in pink crepe trimmed with two egrets: **Rose Valois.** Coiffure: **Henry Durand.** Black suede wedge pumps: **Costa.**
Décor: **Georges Wakhevitch.**

59. Heim Jeunes Filles

Long-sleeved afternoon dress in blue-and-white striped Petillault linen (synthetic). High shawl collar, three-button bodice belted in white leather. Use of contrasting stripes for full skirt.
Big white raffia hat with striped bow: **Jacques Heim.** Coiffure: **Jacques Cohen.** White wedge sandals with blue leather piping: **Hellstern.** White leather handbag with gold nailhead flap: **Lalo.** White linen gloves with blue saddle stitching.
Décor: **André Dignimont.**
References: *Marie-France,* August 7, 1946, p. 11. *Plaire,* Album de Luxe, No. 3, 1946, p. 165. *Fémina,* July-August 1946, p. 102.

60. Henry à la Pensée

Two-piece afternoon dress in pale beige crepe (synthetic). Tunic top with deep V-neck, three-quarter-length raglan sleeves, draped basque gathered in a back "pouf" over the pleated skirt. Self-belt with gold buckle.
Plum suede toque trimmed with lilac and field flowers, green veil: **Jane Blanchot.** Coiffure: **Desfossés.** Plum suede shoes: **Gelé.** Plum suede handbag: **Henry à la Pensée.** Long plum suede gloves.
Décor: **Georges Wakhevitch.**

61. Henriette Beaujeu

Back-buttoned crepe de chine dress printed with butterflies and daisies (Ducharne). Bolero effect, deep decolleté with a rosette of white lace. Short puffed turned-back sleeves. A finely pleated bias band trims the neck, sleeves, and pockets. Full skirt with back-tied sash.
Large white straw hat trimmed with roses and green velvet ribbon: **Rose Valois.** Coiffure: **Pourrière.** Stitched black suede ankle-strap wedge shoes: **Grezy.** Handbag (missing): **Suviane.** Long black suede gloves: **Hermès.**
Décor: **Louis Touchagues.**
Reference: *Plaire,* Summer 1946, Special Collection issue, p. 65.

63. Blanche Issartel

Coat and dress in light navy wool. Draped shoulders and lapels inside wide V-shaped découpe. Fitted waist marked by self-fabric covered chain. Deep back pleats.
Hat (missing): **Odette Colson.** Coiffure: **Gisèle Dumatras.** Shoes (missing): **Drettas.**
Décor: unknown.

58

57

61

63

64

65

66

67

68

70

64. Jeanne Lafaurie

Fitted dress in black crepe (synthetic) with trapeze neckline. Elbow-length kimono sleeves. Asymmetrical drape with fullness brought from the back of the skirt.
Black straw picture hat trimmed with bow and shirred black tulle: **Legroux.** Coiffure: **Jean Clément.** Black suede ankle-strap sandals: **Casale.** Parasol (missing): **Jade.** Black tulle elbow-length gloves: **Dumont.**
Décor: **Jean Saint-Martin.**

65. Jeanne Lanvin

Navy blue organdy afternoon dress. V-neck top with short sleeves. Deep scalloped bertha collar and cuffs made of bias bands of white organdy and openwork embroidery. Full skirt.
Flower toque: **Jeanne Lanvin.** Coiffure: **Rambaud.** Navy leather and suede sling sandals: **Hellstern.**
Gloves (missing): **Faré.**
Décor: **Jean Saint-Martin.**

66. Germaine Lecomte. "Récital"

Back-buttoned ivory silk faille dress with puffed sleeves. Horizontally pleated bodice, square-necked with gold bee clips. Gathered peplum over straight skirt.
Large white straw hat lined in black velvet with black velvet bow: **Rose Valois.** Coiffure: **Jean Clément.** Black suede sling wedges with ivory leather piping: **Grezy.** Long black suede gloves with white embroidery: **Vaisman.** Jewel clips: **Roleine.**
Décor: **Joan Rebull.**
Reference: *Plaire.* No. 7-8, 1946, p.22

67. Lucien Lelong

White (synthetic) crepe two-piece dress with three-quarter sleeves, wide revers. V-neck, wrapped tunic and wrapped skirt with side draping, sashed at the waist.
Coiffure: **Charbonnier.** White suede shoes: **Elie.** Short white gloves: unknown. Parasol (missing): **Vedrennes.** Plum color handbag: **Model.**
Décor: **Georges Wakhevitch.**

68. Mad Carpentier

Dress and jacket ensemble. White (synthetic) linen waist-length blouson. Two ceramic buttons. A deep fold from the waist forms extended shoulders. Full sleeves with gussets. Navy-and-white chevron pattern (synthetic) linen skirt.
White artificial straw hat, linen crown trimmed with white moiré bow: **Albouy.** Coiffure: **Guillaume.** Beige leather sandals with navy blue heels: **Maniatis.** Navy suede gloves.
Décor: **Jean Saint-Martin.**

69. Maggy Rouff

White horizontally pleated organdy dress. Fitted bodice buttoned to the waist. Short puffed sleeves. Peter Pan collar, full skirt.
Hat (missing): **Legroux.** White leather shoes laced in black velvet: **Casale.**
Décor: **Georges Wakhevitch.**

70. Lucile Manguin

White crepe entirely draped dress (synthetic). Kimono batwing sleeves, full skirt widely sashed at the waist.
Hat (missing): **Lucile Manguin.** Coiffure: **Alex Tonio.**
Shoes (missing): **Schifferson.**
Décor: **Louis Touchagues.**

71. Marcelle Alix

Ensemble. Coat in yellow-and-gray printed crepe (synthetic) with yellow and pink gathered jersey (synthetic) front panels. Dress with long sleeves in pink jersey, deep V-neck, midriff with stitched draping to the hipbone. Full skirt.
Hat (missing): **Claude Saint-Cyr.** Coiffure: **Roger Para.**
Wedge sandals in silver leather and lizard: **Elias.**
Décor: **Georges Wakhevitch.**
References: *Plaire.* 1946 Collection Album, p. 57 and 188.
Silhouette, May 1946, p. 87.

72. Martial & Armand

Coat and dress ensemble. Navy wool crepe coat with stand-up collar. Side opening over a dress with two double ruffles in red-and-blue striped faille; matching striped belt.
Fabric: **Bianchini Ferier** (synthetic and silk). Large straw hat with navy faille bow: **Blanch & Simone.** Coiffure: **Villamor & Gille.** Side-laced platform shoes in red leather with navy stitching: **Bertili.**
Décor: **Louis Touchagues.**

69

72

71

72

73   74

73. Mendel

Apple green (synthetic) crepe dress with square neck, fitted bodice, and short accordion-pleated sleeves trimmed with a bow. Flared skirt with hip draping held by side bows and with inserts of accordion pleats.
Green felt hat with bow: **Nelly Levasseur.** Coiffure: **Desfossés.** Shoes (missing): **Casale.** Accessories (missing): **Choses d'Art.** Mustard suede gloves: **Hermès.**
Décor: unknown.

74. Molyneux

Dress in navy and white checked twill (synthetic). Fitted bodice, bow-trimmed short puffed sleeves, full bias skirt with cummerbund. Navy faille petticoat with ruching.
Wide rolled-brim hat in shiny navy straw with white faille lining: **Molyneux.** Coiffure: **Desfossés.** Shoes (missing): **Gillet.** Navy leather handbag with flap: **Model.** Elbow-length gloves in blue leather.
Décor: **André Dignimont.**

75. Charles Montaigne

Pale yellow wool princess dress, three-quarter-length sleeves, wrapover fichu tied in the back over plastron insert with fagotting detail. Gored skirt.
Hat (missing): **Claude Saint-Cyr.** Coiffure: **Alex Tonio.** Navy leather wedge strapped sandals: **Grezy.** Navy blue leather handbag: **Desrues.** Navy blue leather gloves.
Décor: **Louis Touchagues.**
Reference: *Plaire*, 1946, Special Collection issue, p. 55.

76

75

76. Nina Ricci

Dress and jacket ensemble. Loose jacket in brick-red linen. Scalloped lapels and pockets edged in navy soutache. Dress in navy crepe (synthetic) belted in red. Skirt with pleated panel in front.
Navy (artificial) straw hat with felt crown, navy pompon: **Maude & Nano.** Coiffure: **Pourrière.** Navy leather platform sling back sandals: **Léandre.** Navy blue crepe gloves.
Décor: **Louis Touchagues.**
Reference: *L'Officiel*, April 1946, p. 88.

77. O'Rossen

Coat and dress ensemble. Loose black (synthetic) crepe coat lined in bright yellow crepe with black swallow print. Long-sleeved dress in matching yellow print worked on the bias; self cord belt.
Rolled-brim black straw hat with yellow velvet back bow: **Rose Descat.** Coiffure: **AGG.** Black suede sandals with straps piped in gold leather: **Greco.** Black suede gloves: **Hermès.**
Décor: **Georges Douking.**

78. Paquin

Black wool shawl-collared dress. Black faille hip drape falling over straight skirt. Four covered buttons.
Small pink felt hat with white dove and black veil: **Paquin.** Coiffure: **Jean-Pierre.** Black suede sling-back, open-toed sandals piped in pink leather: **Richomme.** Pink kid gloves with black dots: **Faré.** Black suede double-pouch bag.
Décor: **Jean Saint-Martin.**
References: *Fémina*, 1946, p. 77. *La Femme Chic*, 1946 Special Collection issue, p. 32. *Plaire*, Album de Luxe, 1946, No. 3, p. 89. Bibliography: catalogue, Paquin exhibition, Lyon. Musée historique des Tissues, 1989-1990, p. 91, No. 125.

79. Jean Patou. "Provocante"

Ensemble. Three-quarter jacket in raspberry wool jersey, three ceramic buttons. Raglan sleeves with gussets and wide black wool cuffs. Fitted black wool dress, small notched collar, black wool and pink dot sash, falling over flared skirt.
Black stitched tulle picture hat with two black velvet fringed feathers: **Jean Patou.** Coiffure: **Luzic.** Black suede ankle-strap sandals with leather heels: **Maniatis.**
Décor: **Joan Rebull.**

80. Raphaël

Navy wool suit. Fitted double-breasted jacket, velvet shawl collar, set-in sleeves, velvet trimmed pockets. White silk ottoman vest. Straight skirt.
Coolie hat in pale green straw with two red and black feathers: **Raphaël.** Coiffure: **Antonio.** Shoes (missing): **Léandre.** Navy suede handbag: **Lalo.**
Décor: **Jean Saint-Martin.**

81. Georgette Renal

Coat and dress ensemble in pink-and-white printed linen. Short-sleeved redingote (synthetic) over ivory (synthetic) satin crepe dress with fitted top and wide decolleté. Gathered skirt with bands of matching print.
Fabric: **R. Périer.** Hat in ivory felt with pink ottoman crown and white feather: **Maude & Nano.** Coiffure: **Georgius.** White leather sandals: **Penthesilée.** Gloves (missing): **Faré.**
Décor: **André Dignimont.**
Reference: *Silhouette*, May 1946, p. 95.

76

77

78

79

80

81

82

83

84

85

86

87

82. Marcel Rochas

Black wool dress (Rodier). Notched collar, front buttoning, and tucked waist. Straight skirt with three asymmetrical tiers. Ivory satin toque veiled in black lace with lace knots on the side: **Legroux.** Coiffure: **Gervais.** Shoes (missing): **Léandre.** White kid and black lace gloves: **Rochas.** Black suede bag.
Décor: **Georges Wakhevitch.**
References: *La Femme Chic*, 1946 Special Collection issue, p. 37. *Plaire*, Album de Luxe, No. 3, 1946, p. 80. *Album de la Mode du Figaro*, Summer 1946, p. 101.

83. Robert Piguet

Jacket and dress ensemble. Three-quarter box jacket in pink and gray heather tweed. Cape effect from round shoulder yoke. Straight black wool crepe dress.
Black straw picture hat with double black organza edge and white flower: **Paulette.** Coiffure: **Antonio.** Platform black suede pumps: **Argence.** Pearl necklace.
Décor: **Louis Touchagues.**
References: *Plaire*, Album de Luxe, No. 3, 1946, p. 84. drawing by P. Simon. *Album de la Mode du Figaro*, 1946, p. 106. *Vogue*, 1946, p. 104 (Paulette's hat).

84. Rosevienne

Long-sleeved afternoon dress in periwinkle-and-navy checked twill (synthetic). Notched collar over white lace jabot. Draped skirt with apron front panel.
Picture hat in black (artificial) straw with navy velvet ribbon: **Rosevienne.** Coiffure: **Desfossés.** Shoes (missing): **Grezy.**
Décor: **Louis Touchagues.**
Reference: *Plaire*, Album de Luxe, No. 3, 1946, p. 180.

85. Schiaparelli

Turquoise (synthetic) crepe dress. Stand-up collar. An epaulette effect over short sleeves becomes two back panels that tie around the waist. Full skirt.
Small black (artificial) straw hat with turquoise crepe bow in front: **Schiaparelli.** Coiffure: **Marc Ruyer.** Yellow suede ankle-strap shoes: **Casale.** Long yellow suede gloves: **Faré.** Parasol (missing): **Vedrennes.**
Décor: **André Dignimont.**

86. Véra Borea

Lilac (artificial) crepe dress with cuffed three-quarter sleeves. Wrapped top. Two gilt and strass clips at the shoulder hold a pleated drape that continues down to the hem and up to the waist in back.
Black straw pillbox with veil tied around the neck: **Maude & Nano.** Coiffure: **Simoneau.** Shoes (missing): **Codréanu.** Handbag (missing): **Model.** Long black suede gloves: **Paulette.** Clips: **Desrues.**
Décor: **Georges Wakhevitch (?).**

87. Madeleine Vramant

Long-sleeved dress in bois de rose satin. Fitted bodice, round yoke, small shirt collar. At the hips, two panels tied in back fall over the full skirt.
Small natural straw bonnet with grosgrain bow and gray bird-of-paradise feathers: **Suzanne Talbot.** Coiffure: **Lautier.** Shoes (missing): **Georgette.** Three-strand pearl necklace.
Décor: **Georges Wakhevitch.**

88. Worth

Black matte crepe belted tunic and straight skirt. Square neck, trimmed at the shoulders by two écru linen embroidered flowers with green bias and écru braid trim. Ruched trim on basque and skirt.
Hat (missing): **Maude Roser.** Coiffure: **Gabriel Fau.** Black leather and suede sandals: **Casale.** Gloves (missing): **Faré.**
Fabric: **Coudurier, Fructus, Descher.**
Décor: **Georges Douking.**
References: *La Femme Chic*, Summer 1946, p. 18, drawing by P. Mourgue. *Plaire*, Album de Luxe, No. 3, 1946, p. 307.

89. Agnès Drecoll

Cocktail dress in black silk faille and black point d'esprit. Square neck with two bows. Hip drape tied on the side. Layered skirt.
Hat (missing): **Gaby Mono.** Coiffure: **Prévost.** Black suede and leather sandals: **Der-Balian.**
Décor: **Georges Wakhevitch.**

90. Marcelle Chaumont

Cape-sleeved cocktail dress in pink wool (Lesur). Draped bodice, deep V-neck, green wool belt. Full skirt with wavy tuck detail. Big old-rose picture hat with pink grosgrain ribbon: **Le Monnier.** Coiffure: **Lebreuilly.** Pistachio leather shoes piped in pink: **Bunting.**
Décor: **Louis Touchagues.**
References: *L'Art et la Mode*, Spring-Summer 1946, p. 92.

88

89

84

90

92

93

92. Marcel Dhorme

Black wool cocktail suit. Fitted long basque jacket with black sequin bands. White sequin plastron. Straight skirt with inverted pleat.
Small black ciré toque with black ostrich feathers: **Simone Cange.** Coiffure: **Marcel Birot.** Black suede sling sandals: **Léandre.** Accessories (missing): **Mabille.**
Décor: **Georges Wakhevitch.**

93. Gaston

Dinner dress in matte black (synthetic) crepe. Draped bodice, wrapped elbow sleeves trimmed with pink-and-blue sequined soutache, also used as a belt. Easy skirt gathered in front.
Coiffure: **Henry Durand.** Black suede and gold leather sling-back sandals: **Costa.** Black straw hat with Nile green bird-of-paradise feather. Black crepe gloves.
Décor: **Georges Wakhevitch.**

94

95

94. Jacques Heim

Ivory crepe long evening dress with black sequins and black lace flower appliqué. Cuffed pleated short sleeves. Gored skirt with hip tucks flared at hem.
Fabric: **Coudurier, Fructus & Desher** (synthetic). Hat in black shirred and sequined tulle with black veil: **Jacques Heim.** Coiffure: **Jacques Cohen.** Shoes (missing): **Hellstern.** Bag (missing): **Lalo.** Ivory crepe parasol embroidered in black: **Ladousse.** Black sequined tulle mittens: **Jacques Heim.** Embroidery: **Bataille.**
Décor: **Jean Saint-Martin.**

95. Hermès

At-home déshabillé with big puffed sleeves in striped matte and shiny pink, blue, and mauve taffeta. Wrapped top with notched collar and wide mauve and fuschia sash. Culotte skirt in front.
Fabric: **Bianchini Férier.** Coiffure: **Antoine.** Matching fabric wedge sandals: **Hermès.**
Décor: **Joan Rebull.**
Reference: *Vogue "Libération"* issue, January 1945, p. 102 (fabric).

96. Blanche Issartel

Cocktail ensemble. Long-sleeved flared tunic with stand-up collar, in black ciré ribbon horizontal bands. Straight skirt with inverted back pleats in black (synthetic) crepe.
Fabric: **Pierray.** Black straw toque with side trim of roses and black lace veil: **Odette Colson.** Coiffure: **Gisèle Dumatras.** Black suede sling sandals with gold piping: **Drettas.**
Décor: **Georges Wakhevitch.**

97. Lucile Manguin

Ensemble in bottle-green and white star-printed linen (synthetic). Tunic with stitched basque and three-quarter sleeves. Zip front to the waist. Brown leather belt. Straight skirt.
Toast straw hat with flower trim: unknown. Coiffure: **Alex Tonio.** Brown leather wooden-soled wedges: unknown. Belt: **Schifferson.**
Décor: **Louis Touchagues.**

98. Molyneux

Short ermine cape over black crepe sheath dress. Black (faded) crepe toque with black bird-of-paradise feathers.

99. Charles Montaigne

Absinthe-green shantung dress with black dots (synthetic). Three-quarter sleeves. Extended shouldered capelet tied at neck with black velvet ribbon, over square-necked dress with full skirt.
Black (artificial) straw toque with black egrets: **Claude Saint-Cyr.** Coiffure: **Alex Tonio.** Black patent leather and suede sandals: **Grezy.** Accessories (missing): **Desrues.**
Décor: **André Dignimont.**
Reference: *L'Officiel,* April 1946, p. 122.

101. Raphaël

Cocktail dress in gray-blue crepe (synthetic) with elbow-length sleeves. Bias-draped bodice prolonging to form full skirt. Waist defined by basket weave detailing.
Ecru lace hat with flowers: **Raphaël.** Coiffure: **Antonio.** Black suede platform sandals: **Léandre.**
Décor: **Louis Touchagues.**

94

96

97

98

99

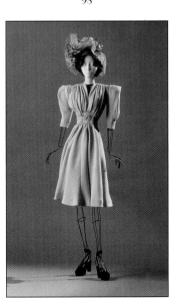

101

104

106

107

109

111

113

104. Véra Borea

Sports suit in pearl gray heather tweed. Three-button jacket, self-belted with gold buckle. Stitched seaming detail and patch pockets. White crepe necktie with gilt V.B. initials. Gored skirt. Bunch of yellow flowers on lapel.
Derby in natural straw with brown grosgrain ribbon and veil: **Maude & Nano.** Coiffure: **Simmoneau.** Brown anklestrap wedge sandals: **Codréanu.** Brown leather and suede bag: **Model.** Flowers: **Judith Barbier.** Buttons and tiepin: **Desrues.**
Décor: **Georges Douking.**

106. Worth

Long ivory crepe dinner dress (synthetic). Elbow-length dolman sleeves, bodice entirely embroidered in bronze and mother-of-pearl sequins. Crossed drape from the waist emphasizes the hips and holds the fullness of the skirt.
Rust tulle coif with brown bird-of-paradise feathers: **Maud Roser.** Coiffure: **Gabriel Fau.** Brown suede and ivory crepe shoes: **Casale.** Rust suede gloves.
Décor: **André Beaurepaire.**

107. Agnès Drecoll

Long dinner dress in mauve-and-white striped taffeta. Fitted bodice, trapeze neckline. Twisted drape across bosom released into fan-shaped pleats over the shoulders and forming short sleeves. Full skirt from side-pointed yoke.
Coiffure: **Prévost.** Garnet necklace and bracelet.
Roses: **Judith Barbier.**
Décor: **Joan Rebull.**

109. Anny Blatt

Long evening dress in beige hand-knitted wool lace backed with tulle and over pink satin sheath. Long full sleeves, deep draped V-neck, ribbon belt in bright green wool crepe. Long gored skirt with fagotting detail.
Coiffure: **Luzic.** Sand suede gloves with ivory leather bow: **Codet & Teillet.**
Décor: **Joan Rebull.**

111. Pierre Balmain

(Missing model remade for the exhibition by Eric Mortensen of Balmain.) Black velvet long-sleeved "sweater" top and ankle-length black crepe skirt entirely bias-draped to center seam. Original 1946 black straw platter hat with egret feathers: **Legroux.** Ermine boa: **Wittelson.** Black satin ankle boots: **Casale.**
Décor: **Georges Geoffroy.**
References: *40 Years of Creation, Pierre Balmain*, Musée de la Mode et du Costume, Palais Galliéra, December-April 1986. cover: drawing by Gruau.

113. Marcelle Dormoy

Short-sleeved long dinner dress in ivory crepe (synthetic). Trapeze neckline. Draped shoulders and bosom held by three embroidered motifs in lamé and pink beading. Draped hip held by same embroidered motifs, falling in two panels and forming a train over the slim, slightly flared skirt.
Coiffure: **Arvet Thouvet.**
Décor: **Jean Cocteau.**

116. Germaine Lecomte. "Soir de Fête"

Long black crepe evening dress (synthetic). Trapeze neckline.
Draped bra in blue and pink satin ribbons embroidered with
bronze sequins and bright red cabochons. Straight skirt slit
on one side with drape around hips tying with the same
embroidered ribbons.
Black egret: **Rose Valois.** Coiffure: **Jean Clément.** Shoes
(missing): **Grezy.** Long pale blue satin gloves: **Vaisman.**
Jewelry: **Régnier.**
Décor: **Christian Bérard.**
References: *L'Art et la Mode*, Spring-Summer 1946, p. 85.
L'Officiel, April 1946, p. 108, drawing by P. Mourgue. *Elle*,
April 30, 1946, p. 21.

117. Lucien Lelong

Short dance dress. Short-sleeved candy-pink crepe top
(synthetic) with draped fichu held by roses. Full skirt in black
surah (synthetic) with fagotted hem.
Coiffure: **Charbonnier.** Black suede shoes piped in black
leather: **Elie.** Pink kid gloves with black suede bows: **Faré.**
Belt: **Mabille.** Flowers: **Judith Barbier.**
Décor: **Georges Wakhevitch.**
References: *Album de la Mode du Figaro*, Summer 1946,
p. 129, drawing by Gruau. *Vogue*, Summer 1946,
p. 140. *Silhouette*, May 1946, p. 61,
drawing by Delfau.

118. Lucile Manguin

Long dinner dress. Long-sleeved
black velvet (synthetic) spencer
with stand-up collar. Full skirt
in champagne organza with
criss-cross of black lace.
Pink taffeta handkerchief
edged in black lace.
Hair ornament, a crown
of wild roses.
Coiffure: **Alex Tonio.**
Décor: **Christian
Bérard.**

116 *117*

118

120

123

127

130

131

135

120. Nina Ricci

Long-sleeved black crepe cocktail dress (synthetic). Front-buttoned bodice, draped square neck extending in a cap effect over the sleeves. Wide drape at hip tied on the side of the wrap-around skirt.

Black straw hat, black satin bow and veil: **Maud & Nano.** Coiffure: **Pourrière.** Black suede sling-back platform sandals: **Léandre.** Black crepe gloves. Jewelry (missing): **Raymond Templier.**

Décor: **Jean Saint-Martin.**

Reference: *Fémina*, May 1946, p. 187, drawing by Delfau.

123. Véra Borea

Sleeveless long evening dress in green and white plaid surah (synthetic). Deep V-neck with "modesty." Two long bias panels from the shoulders continue to form the fullness of the skirt and the train.

Coiffure: **Simmoneau.** Drop earrings in cutout gilt: **Desrues.** Belt (missing).

Décor: **Jean Cocteau.**

Reference: *Vogue*, Summer 1946, p. 140.

127. Annek

At-home déshabillé in pink faille (synthetic) with silk embroidery on sleeves and hem. Big bouffant sleeves. Wide turquoise figured-satin ribbon belt.

Coiffure: **Antonio.**

Décor: **Joan Rebull.**

130. Bruyère

Long princess-shape evening dress in garnet-and-white floral jacquard satin (Coudurier, Fructus, Desher). Décolleté and shoulder straps embroidered with rhinestones and blue beads. Draped bosom. Gored skirt.

Mantilla in brown tulle (missing): **Bruyère.** Coiffure: **Luzic.** Shoes in matching fabric and bordeaux leather: **Hellstern.**

Décor: **Jean-Denis Malclès.**

References: *Album de la Mode du Figaro*, Summer 1946, p. 132, drawing by Mourgue. *L'Art et la Mode*, Spring-Summer 1946, p. 75.

131. Carven. "Extase"

Halter-necked long evening dress in pale green and pale pink jersey (synthetic). The halter top is twisted and draped, then released to fall in two long panels over the full faille skirt striped in wide bands of white, pale pink, and shades of green. Off-white tulle toque with matching bird-of-paradise feathers.

Coiffure: **Fau.** White fake lizard pumps: **Argence.**

Décor: **Emilio Terry.**

Reference: *Fémina*, May 1946, p. 174, drawing by B. Blossac.

135. Marcelle Dormoy

Pale pink organza long evening dress. Basket weave long-torso bodice continuing to hip and released in a ruffle over the full skirt.

Coiffure: **Arvet Thouvet.**

Décor: **Emilio Terry.**

139. Grès

Long evening dress in bright red organdy (synthetic). Fan-shaped draping forms cap sleeves. Layered full skirt.
Turban and veil in pale green organdy with kingfisher feathers, coral beads, and rhinestones: **Caroline Reboux.**
Coiffure: **Alex Tonio.**
Décor: **Emilio Terry.**

142. Jeanne Lafaurie

Ivory satin strapless long evening dress figured in palest pink and water green (synthetic). Raised floral-motif embroidery of silver lamé, pale pink, and rhinestones on back of very full skirt.
Hair ornament (missing): **Gabrielle.**
Coiffure: **Jean Clément.** Ivory satin shoes: **Casale.** Embroidery: **Rébé.**
Gloves in ivory satin with torsade of silver lamé embroidery at cuff: **Dumont.**
Décor: **Jean Cocteau.**

145. Lucien Lelong. "Faïence"

Strapless long evening dress in ivory tulle reembroidered with gray-blue floral pattern and white sequins, over gray-blue stain underskirt (synthetic). Full gathered skirt.
Coiffure: **Charbonnier.** Pinky-beige pumps: **Elie.** Embroidery: **Bataille.**
Long white kid gloves: **Faré.**
Décor: **Christian Bérard.**
Reference: *Elle.* March 26, 1946, p. 10, photo R. Schall, courtesy UFAC.

139

127

142

145

153

146

146. Mad Carpentier

Long evening dress. Bodice with short draped kimono sleeves in yellow silk chiffon embroidered with blue beads, old rose lamé, and mother-of-pearl sequins. Wide embroidered belt. Full skirt gathered at waist in lilac tulle over cyclamen pink underskirt (synthetic).
Coiffure: **Guillaume.**
Décor: **Jean-Denis Malclès.**

149. Martial & Armand

Pale pink organza evening dress (Bianchini-Ferier) over pink faille (synthetic). Draped bodice, short puffed wrapped sleeves with bow. Corselet of appliqué black lace (Brivet). Full skirt accentuated by folded handkerchief detail. Deep black lace appliqué hem.
Coiffure: **Villamor et Gille.** Shoes (missing): **Bertili.**
Décor: unknown.

151. Charles Montaigne

Evening dress in white dotted swiss (synthetic). Strapped bodice covered by wide draped wrapover fichu. Waist tied with two faille ribbons, pink and pistachio green, tying in back and falling over the full skirt.
Hat (missing): **Sygur.** Coiffure: **Azema.** Long pink faille gloves.
Décor: **Joan Rebull.**

153

149

151

152. Nina Ricci

White cotton organdy long evening dress with bands of machine-embroidered tone-on-tone circles on the full layered skirt. Wrapped draped bodice with layers of ruffles forming short sleeves.
Coiffure: **Pourrière.** Shoes (missing): **Léandre.**
Décor: **Christian Bérard.**

153. O'Rossen

Evening coat in ivory, green, and pink floral jacquard satin of Persian inspiration. Redingote with small shawl collar, front-buttoned, and leg-of-mutton sleeves.
Coiffure: **AGG.**
Décor: **Jean-Denis Malclès.**

154. Paquin

Long evening dress in purple satin (Colcombet). Fitted bodice with shoulder straps. A wide swag of pink and violet satin drapes around the hips and falls over the big full skirt.
Coiffure: **Jean-Pierre.** Purple satin pumps: **Richomme.** Long pink kid gloves: **Faré.** Clip, hair ornament, and bracelet in gold, platinum, and rubies: **Chaumet.**
Décor: **Christian Bérard.**
References: *L'Officiel*, April 1946. *Elle*, March 12, 1946, p. 7. *Elites Françaises*, June 1946, No. 8, p. 34. *Fémina*, May 1946, p. 99 (jewelry). Bibliography: catalogue, Paquin exhibition, Lyon, Musée Historique des Tissus, p. 91, No. 126.

155. Jean Patou. "Fleurs de Mal"

Evening dress. Short cap-sleeved bodice in black tulle (synthetic) embroidered in black sequins. Candy-pink wrap-around crepe (synthetic) slim skirt, asymmetrically draped. Loose pleated panel side back. High fez of black egret feathers: **Jean Patou.** Coiffure: **Luzic.** Pink crepe and black leather ankle-wrapped sandals: **Maniatis.**
Décor: **André Beaurepaire.**
References: *Album de la Mode du Figaro*, Summer 1946, p. 141, Gruau. *Silhouette*, May 1946, p. 57, drawing by Gruau. *Elle*, June 21, 1946, p. 10. *L'Officiel*, June 1946, p. 79, drawing by P. Mourgue. *Vogue*, Summer 1946, p. 81, photo Horst.

161. Balenciaga

Raspberry satin (synthetic) long evening dress with tiny collar, long narrow sleeves, and full skirt.
Embroidery of pearls and ruby beads.
Embroidered pillbox: **Balenciaga.** Coiffure: **Georges.**
Décor: **André Beaurepaire.**

163. Bruyère

Hooded long evening dress in pale pink tulle (synthetic). Fitted bodice with gathered ruffles forming short sleeves. A narrow matching cord wraps around the body, making a corselet waist. The same cord is used at the hem of the full skirt and around the hood.
Coiffure: **Luzic.** Shoes (missing): **Georgette.**
Jewelry: **Mauboussin.**
Décor: **Christian Bérard.**

152

153

154

155

161

163

165

166

165. Marcelle Dormoy

Long evening dress in greige organza printed with giant cherry bows. Matching stole. Bodice has two gathered straps and is finely draped to the hips. Full skirt.
Coiffure: **Arvet-Thouvet.**
Décor: **Emilio Terry.**

166. Jacques Fath. "Caran d'Ache"

Long black velvet evening sheath buttoned down the front. Small stand-up collar, long narrow sleeves. From the knee, a wide flounce of pink satin overlaid with sequined tulle (synthetic) and held by a black velvet ribbon and bow. Platter hat in sequined tulle with black velvet bow and black egret feathers: **Jacques Fath.** Coiffure: **Gervais.** Black suede platform pumps: **Jourdan.** Black sequined bag: **Jacques Fath.** Black velvet gloves.
Décor: **Emilio Terry.**
References: *Album de la Mode du Figaro*, Summer 1946, p. 140. *Silhouette*, May 1946, p. 33. *Elle*, April 2, 1946, p. 12. *Fémina*, May 1946, p. 118. *L'Art et la Mode*, Spring-Summer 1946, p. 82.

167. Gaston

Ivory satin long evening dress. The long-sleeved fitted bodice has a full gathered peplum with embroidery of white and gold pearls and sequins. Big full skirt.
White egret feather hair ornament: **Geneviève Marma.**
Coiffure: **Henry Durand.** White satin pumps: **Costa.**
Décor: **Christian Bérard.**

167

178

156

168. Grès

Black silk organdy long evening dress. Long sleeves, fitted bodice tucked through the waist. Full skirt split in front over bright green organdy underskirt.
Black organdy shoulder-length veil with lophophore (Tibetan pheasant) feathers: **Caroline Reboux.** Coiffure: **Alex Tonio.**
Décor: **Christian Bérard.**

169. Jacques Heim

Long mink evening coat. Long evening dress in white Bourdelin crepe (synthetic). Bodice is draped over the bosom and has string straps. Narrow skirt with front fullness and network embroidery of ivory velvet and beaded tassels at hips.
Coiffure: **Jacques Cohen.** Bag (missing): **Lalo.** Embroidery: **Bataille.**
Décor: **Christian Bérard.**

170. Blanche Issartel

Evening coat in ivory satin patterned in silver, an Italian Renaissance inspiration. Draped capelet effect. Inset corselet waist. Gored skirt. Worn over long gold lamé sheath.
Fabric (synthetic): **Hurel.** Hair ornament of twisted bronze cords: **Odette Colson.** Coiffure: **Gisèle Dumatras.** Platform sandals in white and gold leather: **Drettas.** White suede gloves.
Décor: **André Beaurepaire.**

173. Lucien Lelong

Evening ensemble. Orange crepe (synthetic) draped cutaway jacket and long slim skirt with small front slit. One-shoulder black crepe top.
Coiffure: **Charbonnier.** Shoes (missing): **Elie.** Black suede gloves: **Faré.** Self belt: **Mabille.** Jewelry: **Boivin.**
Décor: **Christian Bérard.**
References: *Vogue*, Summer 1946, p. 79, drawing by Eric. *Elle*, April 2, 1946, p. 13, drawing by Gruau. *Album de la Mode du Figaro*, Summer 1946, p. 97, drawing by Gruau. *American Vogue*, April 15, 1946, drawing by Eric.

174. Mad Carpentier

Long evening dress in mauve-and-white striped taffeta (synthetic). Leg-of-mutton sleeves. Bias-draped V-neck.
Over the full gored skirt, a triangle of white satin embroidered in black lace and jet, held at the waist in front and draping low in back.
Coiffure: **Guillaume.**
Décor: **Christian Bérard.**

178. Mendel. "Rose de France"

Full-length ermine cape lined in pale pink satin (synthetic). Matching pink satin evening dress, the strapless bodice and full skirt embroidered in a scroll pattern of old-gold sequins.
Coiffure: **Desfossés.** Embroidery: **Gaby.** Pale pink kid gloves: **Hermès.**
Décor: **Christian Bérard.**
Reference: *Fémina*, May 1946, p. 170, drawing by Gruau.

168

169

170

173

174

178

180

182

181

180. Nina Ricci

Black satin evening dress (synthetic). Full leg-of-mutton sleeves. Fitted bodice with set-in yoke of pale pink satin embroidered with old-gold sequins. Deep décolleté over black satin "modesty." Full skirt over longer pink satin underskirt (synthetic).
Coiffure: **Pourrière.** Ivory satin pumps: **Léandre.**
Black satin gloves embroidered with sequins.
Décor: **André Beaurepaire.**

181. Paquin

White chiffon wedding dress with full skirt worked in bands of ruching. Long-sleeved fitted bodice closed with tiny covered buttons. White satin ribbon at waist trimmed with camelias.
Pillbox and veil in tulle and écru lace: **Paquin.**
Coiffure: **Jean-Pierre.** White satin and white leather pumps: **Richomme.** Ecru lace gloves.
Décor: **André Beaurepaire.**
Bibliography: Paquin exhibition, Lyon, Musée Historique des Tissus, December 1989-March 1990, catalogue, p. 91, No. 1276.

182. Jean Patou. "Nocturne"

Black organza over pink satin long evening dress. V-neck fitted bodice with pleats forming cap sleeves and becoming a cowl in back. Full skirt with deep inverted pleats, embroidered with large jet and sequin chrysanthemums.
Hair ornament of one pink, one black egret feather: **Jean Patou.** Coiffure: **Luzic.**
Décor: **Jean-Denis Malclès.**
Reference: *Silhouette*, May 1946, p. 83, drawing by Gruau.

180

184. Georgette Renal

Evening dress. Short-sleeved, V-necked wrapped bodice in white satin (synthetic) with smocking on shoulders. Full skirt in white tulle trimmed with widening bands of white satin. White satin underskirt.
Hair ornament of black velvet ribbon and white bird-of-paradise feathers. Shoes (missing): **Penthesilée.**
Gloves (missing): **Faré.**
Décor: **Joan Rebull.**
Reference: *Marie-France,* May 1, 1946, p. 8.

185. Marcel Rochas

Black velvet strapless bodice with pink satin rose. Full skirt of layered petals in black tulle over black faille petticoat (synthetic).
Coiffure: **Gervais.** Shoes (missing): **Léandre.** Necklace and egret in diamonds: **Boucheron.** Pink suede gloves.
Décor: **Christian Bérard.**
Reference: *Fémina,* May 1946, p. 99 (jewelry).

186. Robert Piguet

Striped slate-gray and white rustic linen evening dress (synthetic). Cap-sleeved sheath with crossover draping at the hip and navy grosgrain ribbon tied on one side. Horizontally striped bodice contrasting with vertically striped skirt.
Navy jersey turban with three egret feathers in navy, pistachio green and white: **Paulette.** Coiffure: **Antonio.** Navy suede pumps: **Argence.**
Décor: **Christian Bérard.**
References: *America Vogue,* April 1, 1946, p. 173 and *Vogue,* Summer 1946, p. 17, photo Horst. *Elle,* July 23, 1946, p. 3.

187. Schiaparelli

Long-sleeved evening dress with pink satin fitted wrapover bodice and flared skirt made of wavy horizontal bands in shades of fuchsia, lilac, and violet. Between each band, metallic embroidery covered with a zigzag of white thread (synthetic).
Coiffure: **Marc Ruyer.** Shoes (missing): **Casale.** Pink kid gloves: **Faré.** Embroidery: **Lesage.** Diamond, ruby, and platinum tiara, epaulettes, and belt: **Van Cleef & Arpels.**
Décor: **Christian Bérard.**
Reference: *Fémina,* May 1946, p. 99.

189. Worth

Ivory silk damask evening dress with large floral pattern. Fitted bodice with wide straps, entirely embroidered in sequins and gold thread in a twig and stylized flower motif. Two long pointed side panels of the same embroidery fall over the full skirt.
Coiffure: **Gabriel Fau.**
Décor: **Emilio Terry.**
References: *Silhouette,* May 1946, p. 66, drawing by Gruau. *Fémina,* May 1946, p. 116.

193. Mad Carpentier

Black and silver paisley-pattern silk brocade evening coat. Full-skirted redingote shape, stand-up collar, large puffed sleeves with extended shoulder effect.
Toque in black velvet and tulle embroidered with sequins and jet and trimmed with feathers: **Albouy.** Coiffure: **Jacqueline.** Décor: **Emilio Terry.**

184

185

186

187

189

193

194

196

198

200

201

203

194. Maggy Rouff

White (synthetic) jersey long evening dress. Bodice gathered from corded epaulette effect. Long fully gathered skirt with a sari-skirt panel.
Shoes (missing): **Casale.** Gold and precious stone necklace, cuff bracelet, and jeweled cord belt: **Van Cleef & Arpels.**
Décor: **Christian Bérard** (theater box).
Reference: *Fémina*, Spring 1946, p. 98 (jewelry).

196. Calixte

Long bare-backed evening dress in vertical bias panels of pink, blue, lavender, cream, black, and gray rustic linen.
Cowl drape worn as a hood.
Coiffure: **Antonio.**
Décor: **Emilio Terry.**

198. Mad Carpentier

Black crepe evening dress (synthetic). Bodice with wide black velvet cape collar (synthetic) embroidered with a band of tulle, sequins, and jet. Three-quarter puffed sleeves. Straight skirt.
Hair ornament of black velvet ribbon and bird-of-paradise feathers: **Albouy.** Coiffure: **Azema.**
Décor: **Christian Bérard** (half figure for theater box).

200.

Unattributed model. Ref. Catalogue USA. (Hats). Brown tulle evening dress (synthetic). Boat-necked bodice. Long sleeves. At the hips, a pleated drape forming a pouf in back. Full skirt.
Hair ornament in brown tulle veiling with brown and white bird-of-paradise feathers: **Annie.** Necklace in gold metal and rhinestones. Coiffure: **Jean Clément.**
Décor: **Christian Bérard** (half figure for theater box).

201. Grès

Evening coat in rust silk velvet. Fan-draped bodice, the draping continuing to form huge puffed sleeves to the elbow.
Turban in matching velvet with lophophore (Tibetan pheasant) feathers: **Caroline Reboux.**
Décor: **Christian Bérard** (half figure for theater box).

203. Carven

Lilac satin evening dress (synthetic). Strapless top with gathers continuing over the hips and trimmed with forget-me-nots. Full skirt.
Hair ornament of forget-me-nots, flowerets, and pink egret feathers: **Denis Chabaud.** Coiffure: **Lebreuilly.**
Décor: **Christian Bérard** (half figure for theater box).

204.

Unattributed model. Ref. Catalogue USA. (Hats). Yellow rustic linen evening dress (synthetic). Unpressed pleated bodice with extended shoulders held at the waist by a twisted selfbelt. Full skirt.
Almond-green taffeta toque trimmed with lilac and green ostrich feathers: **Eneley Sœurs.** Long black satin gloves.
Décor: **Emilio Terry** (half figure).

207. Carven
Evening dress in navy tulle with white sequins and cutout over-embroidered white piqué. The bodice is mounted on navy faille. Tied shoulder straps, puff sleeves, and full skirt. White jasmine and ostrich feather hair ornament: **Germaine Bouche.** Coiffure: **Jean Clément.**
Décor: **Christian Bérard** (half figure for theater box).

208.
Unattributed model. Ref. Catalogue USA. (Hats). Black velvet three-quarter-sleeved bodice draped around the shoulders. Full black taffeta skirt (synthetic).
Portrait hat in black velvet trimmed with black tulle and white guipure lace flowers: **Gilbert Orcel.** Coiffure: **Guillaume.**
Décor: **Christian Bérard** (half figure for theater box).
References: *Fémina*, May 1946, p. 201 (hat).

196

204

207

208

210

213

210. Jungmann

White rabbit jacket.
Gold-and-silver braided lamé ribbon turban with black bird-of-paradise feather: **Jane Blanchot.** Coiffure: **Guillaume.** Long black suede gloves.
Décor: **Christian Bérard** (half figure for theater box).

211. Pierre Balmain

Strapless pale pink silk satin evening dress. Silver sequin and rhinestone embroidered bra effect. Long mittens in matching embroidery. Full skirt.
Turban in pink satin with black egret feather: **Janette Colombier.**
Décor: **Christian Bérard** (half figure for theater box).

213.

Unattributed model. Ref. Catalogue USA. (Hats). Black (synthetic) crepe evening dress. Draped bodice à l'antique. Flared skirt.
Toque in black raffia with uncurled black ostrich feather: **Maud & Nano.** Coiffure: **Guillaume.** Ermine stole: **Reine d'Angleterre.**
Décor: **Christian Bérard** (half figure for theater box).

216

211

214. Lucien Lelong

Strapless ivory satin evening dress (synthetic). Cutaway
tunic-length cuffed bodice draped over the bosom.
Straight skirt.
Black tulle and looped black satin ribbon hat with black egret
feathers: **Maud Roser.** Long black suede gloves: **Faré.**
Décor: **Christian Bérard.**
Reference: *Fémina*, May 1946, p. 119, drawing by Gruau.

215. Madeleine Vramant

White matte jersey evening dress (synthetic). Corsage with
vertical and horizontal finely pleated draping.
Crown of white egrets and bow of white satin: **Nelly
Levasseur.** Coiffure: **Desfossés.**
Décor: **Christian Bérard** (half figure for theater box).

216.

Unattributed model. Ref. Catalogue USA. (Hats). Strapless
pale yellow satin evening dress (synthetic). Peplumed bodice
embroidered in black sequins and jet. Full skirt.
Matching turban with three white bird-of-paradise feathers:
Paulette. Coiffure: **Georgel.** White ermine stole: **Révillon.**
Long black suede gloves.
Décor: **Christian Bérard** (half figure for theater box).

218. Alice Thomas

White satin evening dress (synthetic). Long-sleeved puckered
"sweater" top with silver sequins. Narrow skirt.
Hair ornament (missing): **Simone Cange.** Coiffure: **Marcel
Birot.**
Décor: **Christian Bérard** (half figure for theater box).

220. Marcelle Alix

Evening dress in puffs of blue, yellow, pink, and green tulle.
Hair ornament of pink and blue bird-of-paradise feathers held
by a mother-of-pearl flower: **Suzanne Talbot.** Coiffure: **Roger
Para.** Long gold mesh gloves.
Décor: **Christian Bérard** (half figure for theater box).

221. Charles Montaigne

Pink and gold taffeta lamé evening dress, scallop pattern.
Shallow V-neck, fitted bodice with large draped shoulder cape.
Six self-covered buttons. Full skirt.
Hat (missing): **Sygur.** Coiffure: **Marc Royer.** Accessories
(missing): **Chevrier.** Long black chiffon gloves.
Décor: **Christian Bérard** (half figure for theater box).

214

215

216

218

220

221

222

223

224

225

226

227

222. Lucien Lelong

White crepe long evening sheath (synthetic). Long sleeves.
Fan draping over bosom.
Long articulated pendant pin with large yellow sapphire,
gold, diamond, and green beryls: **Boivin.** Hair ornament of two
little gold and diamond cones: **Jean Clément.** Gloves (missing):
Faré.
Décor: **Christian Bérard** (half figure for theater box).

223. Worth

White crepe evening dress (synthetic). Short-sleeved draped
bodice. Full skirt.
"Bird in a Cage" diamond, ruby, and emerald plastron and
hair ornament: **Cartier.** Long almond-green gloves.
Décor: **Christian Bérard** (half figure for theater box).
Reference: *Fémina*, Spring 1946, p. 98, (jewelry).

224. Worth

White crepe evening sheath (synthetic). Short-sleeved
draped corsage. Full skirt.
Ruby and diamond plastron, earrings, bracelet, ring, and
cigarette holder: **Cartier.** Long white suede gloves.
Décor: **Christian Bérard** (half figure for theater box).
Reference: *Fémina*, Spring 1946, p. 98 (jewelry).

225. Paquin

White (synthetic) jersey evening dress with high neck and
extended shoulders. Entirely draped and held in by wide
draped cummerbund. Long white suede gloves.
Necklace, hair ornament, and bracelet in platinum, rubies,
and diamonds: **Chaumet.**
Décor: **Christian Bérard** (half figure for theater box).

226. Molyneux

Short black satin sheath (silk and synthetic). Fitted bodice
with short puffed sleeves. Boat neck.
Necklace in gold and diamonds: **Fontana.** Coiffure: **Desfossés.**
Gloves (missing).
Décor: **Christian Bérard** (half figure for theater box).

227. Bruyère

Evening coatdress in ivory figured silk satin with gold lamé
floral pattern. High crossed neck, full skirt, large bouffant
sleeves.
Gold and diamond necklace: **Mauboussin.** Bird-of-paradise
feather hair ornament (missing): **Bruyère.**
Décor: **Christian Bérard** (half figure for theater box).

228. Marcelle Chaumont

White satin evening dress (synthetic). Fitted bodice with very large shirred puffed sleeves.
Diamond and emerald necklace: **Véver.** Hair ornament.
Emerald green braided velvet ribbon with bow: **Eneley Sœurs.**
Coiffure: **Lebreuilly.**
Décor: **Christian Bérard** (half figure for theater box).

I. Freddy Sport

This house does not appear in the catalogue of the 1946 exhibition but does appear in the British catalogue, London, September 1945.
Sport ensemble. Two-button long fitted jacket in green diagonal wool tweed (Miron). Gold buttons also on martingale, sleeve tabs, and matching vest. Greige wool (Miron) cuffed trousers with waist tucks.
Green felt hat with black veil and black and white feathers.
Green leather platform shoes.
Décor: unknown.
Reference: *L'Art et la Mode.* January-February 1946. p. 31.

II. Marcel Rochas

Wedding dress in ivory satin (synthetic). Long-sleeved fitted bodice. Bow-tied sash. Double flounced basque. Two long panels fall from the shoulders in back over the full skirt and train.
White kid gloves. Ivory satin platform sandals.
Décor: **Jean Cocteau.**

228

I

II

227

165

III

IV

III. Pierre Balmain. "La Sorcière"

Long evening dress in gray tulle embroidered in a scroll pattern with steel gray and rust beads. Full skirt in layers of almond-green and gray tulle with irregular hem.
Gloves in pale yellow suede: **Faré.**
Décor: **Jean Cocteau.**
Bibliography: *40 Years of Creation, Pierre Balmain,* Musée de la Mode et du Costume, Palais Galliéra, December 1985-April 1986. p. 227, photo Kollar.

IV. Blanche Issartel

Dinner ensemble. Cape and straight skirt in black crepe (synthetic). Long-sleeved tunic in red ciré ribbon worked diagonally. Hair ornament of small bright pink carnations and red velvet ribbon.
Décor: **Christian Bérard** (half figure for theater box).
Reference: *Fémina,* May 1946, p. 138 (similar model).

V. Martial & Armand

Evening dress in blue-gray Bianchini Ferier crepe (synthetic) embroidered with brown sequins in a floral motif. Draped short-sleeved bodice with trapeze neckline filled in with tulle. A-line skirt. Mink stole.
Décor: **Christian Bérard** (half figure for theater box).

VI. Unidentified

Afternoon dress in periwinkle blue organdy with white pin dots (synthetic). Bodice with puffed sleeves held by a fuchsia velvet ribbon also used at the waist. Full skirt worked in small flounces gathered at the hips. Pink faille petticoat (synthetic) edged in white lace. Matching wreath of organdy flowers.
Ankle boots in parma suede.
Décor: **André Dignimont.**

VII. Unidentified

Black wool long-sleeved evening sheath. Deep sweetheart neckline. The bust is emphasized by a pink satin drape.
Décor: **Christian Bérard** (half figure for theater box).

VIII. Unidentified

Moss green crepe evening dress (synthetic). Fitted bodice with three-quarter sleeves. Trapeze neckline. Ermine bolero.
Ivory satin hat with black and white egret feathers. Black faille gloves.
Décor: **Christian Bérard** (half figure for theater box).

V

VI

IX. Unidentified

Black (synthetic) jersey evening dress. Draped short-sleeved bodice. Crossed panels at the hip falling over the long skirt. Long embroidered tulle gloves.
Small black clipped feather puff with black bird-of-paradise and pink ostrich feathers.
Décor: **Christian Bérard** (half figure for theater box).

VII

VIII

IX

Missing Models

For the 1990 exhibition **Massaro** remade the shoes for the following models:

2, 4, 5, 10, 15, 18, 21, 23, 33, 43, 54, 55, 63, 73, 74, 80, 82, 84, 86, 87.

III

Epilogue:
The Continuing Story

Colleen Schafroth and Betty Long-Schleif

The Musée de la Mode in Paris, as seen from Tuileries Gardens. The Pavillon Marsan was the location of the Théâtre de la Mode exhibition in both 1945 and 1990.

When the Théâtre de la Mode reopened in 1990 at the Musée des Arts de la Mode within the Louvre in Paris, the fashion world responded with much the same enthusiasm exhibited at the premier opening in 1945.

The collection awed, inspired, and was critically acclaimed in Paris and in subsequent exhibitions in New York; Tokyo; Baltimore; London; Portland, Oregon; Honolulu; and, of course, at Maryhill Museum itself where it has been shown in part since 1995.

Although its success lay mostly in those attributes of fashion that made it so extraordinarily successful back in 1945 and 1946 when it toured Europe and the United States, this latest exhibition also had a strong element of nostalgia. It reminded everyone, especially the French, of those last days of World War II, when they suffered huge deprivations and shortages. For many Europeans, it not only brought painful memories but also those of resilience, pride, and survival. For Americans the exhibit brought back not just memories of the war years, but a shared lifestyle of the late 1940s. Visitors would look upon the Théâtre de la Mode and reminisce about the similarity in the clothes they had worn, many of which were no doubt inspired by the collection and the rest of the French fashion industry.

Perhaps it was as much those memories, the almost tangible essence of a bygone era, that lent an urgency to the idea to bring back the Théâtre de la Mode – to share it once again with the public, and to preserve it for the future. As with the first exhibition, this revival brought together the Parisian fashion houses, designers, artists, fashion authorities, and historians.

Below left: Eliane Bonabel in a 1990 stage decor by Anne Surgers nostalgically holding the poupées *that she designed and worked with in 1944-1946.*

168

The catalyst for the exhibition came in the form of one individual, Susan Train, Paris Bureau Chief of Condé Nast Publications. It was she who gathered around her a circle of friends and associates who became infected by her dream. Some of the original players, those who had created the concept and exhibit in 1945, were also pulled into the project. Robert Ricci, one of the originators of the 1945 enterprise, was sought out for advice. Couture houses still in existence eagerly participated. Surviving artists and set designers were tapped for their experience, their archives, and help.

Perhaps of all the original players, it was Eliane Bonabel, the young artist who originally created the concept of the wire mannequin, who returned to the new project with not only great skill but enthusiasm. Although in her seventies at the time, Eliane Bonabel infused everyone with her *joie de vive* and indefatigable energy. As she did in 1945, Eliane eagerly traveled to New York, and later to Tokyo, to see that her *poupées* were appropriately choreographed.

Scenes from the 1990 Paris opening:

Right: Stanley Garfinkel, the professor of history at Kent State University who "rediscovered" the collection in 1983.

Below: David Seidner with Jackie Jackson, member, Board of Trustees of Maryhill Museum of Art.

Above: Linda Brady Tesner, director of Maryhill Museum of Art, with Eugene Braun-Munk of Editions du May and Susan Train, Condé Nast Publications.

Far right: Anne Surgers, middle, talks with Eliane Bonabel, right.

Right: Patricia del Pra, chief conservator

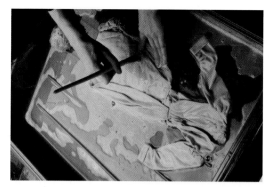

The Théâtre de la Mode mannequins arrived in Paris, two years before their revival, to enter a period of conservation and research. Each surviving mannequin was thoroughly researched, examined, and documented. Under the supervision of Patricia del Pra, chief conservator, the talented staff of Restoration Versailles were given the exacting and time-consuming task of the months-long conservation effort.

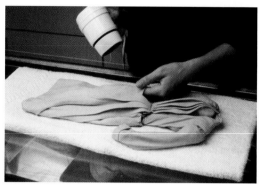

Fabric itself is one of the more fragile and ephemeral products available. Time is its worst enemy, and for many of the garments in the collection, it had cer-

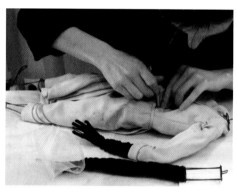

tainly taken its toll. All of them needed careful cleaning. A number of pieces needed more extensive work to arrest fragile fabrics from further decay. This intricate process involved a great deal of careful analysis and study. Threads and fabrics needed for repair had to be carefully dyed and exactingly matched so that work to stabilize fragile ensembles would be invisible.

While the miniature garments were undergoing their treatments, so too were the mannequins. Their wire bodies, heads, and hair were examined and conserved. Where necessary, conservation work was completed to stabilize the armature and fragile plaster heads. Many of the original coiffures needed to be refreshed. This was often painstaking work completed with miniature rollers and pins.

During this process, it had become clear that some of the mannequins in the collection were missing important aspects

Vera Borea's dress (86) undergoes a thorough cleaning before being carefully repositioned on the mannequin. Often the garments were sewed onto the wire armature.

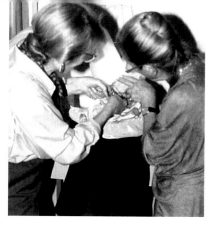

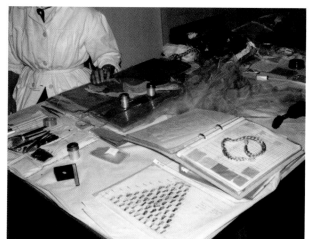

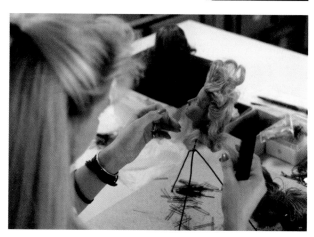

Conservation of the mannequins was done with precision and carefully documented. Above, far right, Eliane Bonabel works on a mannequin before the Paris opening in 1990.

of their ensembles, and that some mannequins were missing entirely. The missing mannequins were assessed through historic photographs, and, after no doubt much Gallic discussion, one dress was considered such a great loss that it was completely recreated for the collection. Fortunately, the original accessories – a 1946 black straw platter hat with egret feathers, the ermine boa by Legroux, and fine suede ankle boots – had survived so that only the gown needed to be replaced. Thus the completely romantic ensemble in black velvet, originally designed by Pierre Balmain from the House of Balmain (111), returned to the Théâtre de la Mode.

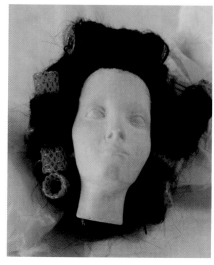

Once restored, the mannequins got their hair done for the first time in over 40 years! In the case of the Maggie Rouff design at left (194), her metal hair was polished, rather than styled.

The jewelry originally made by Van Cleef and Arpels, Chaumet, Cartier, and Bougeron were made with real gemstones set in gold and platinum. They had been returned to their makers at the close of the exhibition in San Francisco in 1946. When this came to light, Susan Train arranged with the House of Chaumet to create replica jewelry accessories for the gown designed by Paquin (225), while the House of Lesage, famous for its metallic, jewel-like embroidery, was persuaded to replicate pieces for three others. Two more were done by the House of Boucheron and House of Goossens.

While this work was going on in the conservation lab, others were researching and re-creating the sets or tableaus in which these newly conserved mannequins would reside at the reopening. Anne Surgers, a talented stage designer, was given the commission to re-create nine of the twelve original sets made for the 1945 European and American tours. The sets chosen included the fabulous Christian Bèrard set that gave the collection its name, *The Théâtre de la Mode*. Also included were sets originally designed by André Beaurepaire, Jean Cocteau, André Dignimont, George Douking, Jean-Denis Malclès, Jean Saint-Martin, Louis Touchagues, and Georges Wakhevitch. The goal was to recreate the atmosphere of the original Théâtre de la Mode.

Simultaneously, fashion researchers, curators, and historians were busy not only researching for the new exhibition of the Théâtre de la Mode, but documenting it, and in the process, ensuring that it would never again be lost to the world of fashion. Ephemera, including original plans, sketches, newspaper clippings, and more were collected and sorted, and copies were made for Maryhill Museum of Art. This information was then distributed through the publication of this book and a video on the Théâtre de la Mode, spearheaded by

When the mannequins travel, the clothed armature is separated from the heads to minimize damage. Each mannequin is carefully wrapped and rests in its own custom-made acid-free box until the next show time.

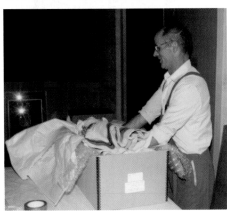

noted scholar Stanley Garfinkel and produced by Telos Video Productions and Trans-Atlantic Video.

Since the renaissance of the original exhibition in Paris in 1990, the collection in whole or in part has appeared at the Metropolitan Museum of Art in New York City, the Fashion Foundation in Tokyo, the Portland (Oregon) Art Museum, the Baltimore Museum of Art, the Imperial War Museum in London, the Maryhill Museum of Art in Goldendale, Washington, the Museum at the Fashion Institute of Technology in New York, and most recently at the University of Hawaii Art Gallery in Honolulu.

From the visitor who is awed by the sheer tenacity and determination of its original creators during a difficult time to a new generation of fashion and stage set designers and artists, the collection has been inspirational.

Indeed even today, over a decade since it reopened in Paris, the collection attracts the attention of fashion historians, new young designers in the field, doll collectors, and the general public, bringing them in droves to Maryhill Museum to see the collection for themselves.

A Lesage replica of the famous Cartier "Bird in a Cage."

Maryhill visitors young and old continue to be mesmerized by the mannequins of Théâtre de la Mode. For over 25 years they were exhibited in glass cases as shown here. Now they may be seen in their traditional décors.

The Finishing Touches...Jewelry in Miniature

(187)

(223)

(225)

(224)

Jewelers, hatmakers, shoemakers...these Paris designers were challenged by the task of creating miniatures for the Théâtre de la Mode mannequins. The pieces of jewelry shown here are reproductions of the original precious items made by Chaumet and Lesage. They were arranged for and underwritten by the Federation Francaise de la Couture.

(187) Gown by Schiaparelli; both original and re-creations of epaulets, tiara and belt by Lesage

(223) Gown by Worth; original jewelry by Cartier was re-created by the House of Boucheron and the House of Goossens in 1990

(225) Gown by Paquin; original and replica jewelry by Chaumet, jeweler since 1780, Paris

(224) Gown by Worth. original jewelry Cartier, replica rhinestone plastron and hair ornaments by the House of Boucheron and the House of Goossens

(222) Gown by Lucien Lelong; original jewelry by Boivin and Jean Clement, replica articulated pendant and head ornaments by Lesage

(194) Gown by Maggy Rouff; original jewelry by Van Cleef & Arpels, replica collar, bracelet and jeweled cord belt by Lesage

(222)

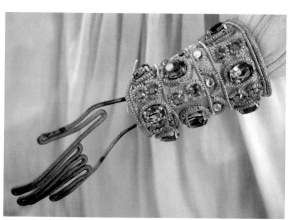

(194)

Coco Chanel once said that discoveries are made to be copied; it is the greatest of compliments. If this is so, then the Théâtre de la Mode has had its sare of compliments.

Strangely enough, even though the Théâtre de la Mode has influenced the world of fashion many times over, it has also had a tremendous impact on the modern world of doll and doll collecting. Although on the surface this seems odd, it shouldn't. After all, dolls have always been associated with fashion. Indeed, the original creators of the Théâtre de la Mode revived for their project a centuries-old tradition of using dolls to disseminate Parisian fashions to the rest of the world.

The manifestations of the collection's inspiration in the doll world appear everywhere. Besides individual creations made at home and for the one-of-a-kind doll market, a variety of doll companies have been inspired as well. Mattel produced a Theater of Fashion series for Barbie®, designed by the American designer, Billy Boy; and Mel Odom created an ensemble for his doll "Gene," based on a dress represented in the collection. Robert Tonner's enthusiasm for the Théâtre de la Mode recently led his company to produce a series of nine special edition dolls on its 16" Tyler Wentworth® fashion doll.

In the same vein, a number of doll clubs from the United States and Europe have enthusiastically embraced the Théâtre de la Mode, presenting conferences and publishing papers that center on the collection as an inspiration and as dolls. Many of these have lobbied for the continued showing of the collection around the United States and Europe. Of all these clubs, it has been the United Federation of Doll Clubs that has most embraced the collection, promoting it among its members and the general public for over a decade.

It is the interest of diverse groups such as these that give light and energy to the Théâtre de la Mode. The latest expressions are simple proof of the power these little ambassadors of fashion and history have had on all our hearts. The future will no doubt bring more exciting new works, all inspired by this timeless collection.

To document the historical accuracy of the Théâtre de la Mode collection, Tonner designers examined the mannequins at Maryhill, taking color samples from the interior seams, which are largely unaltered by environmental fading. Top right, mannequin (56) and Tonner doll.

Bottom right, Tonner doll (146) created for the United Federation of Doll Clubs 2002 convention.

Authors of the Essays

Edmonde Charles-Roux, *writer and member of the Academie Goncourt is also a journalist and in particular was editor-in-chief of French* Vogue *for sixteen years. She is the author of two novels,* Elle, Adrienne *and* Oublier Palerme, *as well as remarkable biographies of Chanel and of Isabelle Eberhardt.*

Herbert R. Lottman *was an American historian known in France and America for his numerous biographies: Albert Camus, Pétain, Flaubert, and Colette. He is also the author of historical works such as* The Writers of the Left Bank *and* The Purge.

Stanley Garfinkel *was a professor of history at Kent State University, and a Harvard graduate, researcher, and oral historian. Known for his recent works on fashion, he is also the author of video documentaries on Christian Dior, Roger Vivier, and the Théâtre de la Mode.*

Nadine Gasc, *curator and head of the fashion and textile department of the Musée des Arts de la Mode, created this department in 1972 for the Musée des Arts Décoratifs. She has been responsible for several fashion exhibitions and their catalogues:* Moments de mode, *1986;* Manuel Canovas, Histoires de mode d'hier et d'aujourd'hui, *1988.*

David Seidner, *photographer, was born in Los Angeles in 1957. He exhibited his work for the first time in Paris in 1978. His portraits and fashion photography and his numerous exhibitions and books, such as* Moments de mode *and* David Seidner, Photographer, *have borne witness to his talent.*

Colleen Schafroth *became the executive director of Maryhill Museum in May 2001. She holds B.A. degrees in English and art as well as an M.A. in art history from Oregon State University. She has authored two books on chess as well as other publications related to Maryhill's collections.*

Betty Long-Schleif *has worked in the museum field since 1977. Armed with an academic background in costume and textile history, she has been responsible for organizing the world travels of the Théâtre de la Mode since 1998. She has published several articles and spoken to numerous groups about this collection.*

Edmonde Charles-Roux, at that time welfare assistant attached to the Fifth Tank Division, was on the Colmar front when Lee Miller took this photo of her. She knew Lee Miller by name; certain friends, artists who had taken refuge in Marseilles, had spoken of her—friends by the names of Christian Bérard, Jean Cocteau, Boris Kochno. Lee Miller, by a strange quirk of circumstance, was to bring her news of these friends who had returned to Paris and were working on the Théâtre de la Mode.

Bérard, Cocteau, and Kochno were putting the final touches on the exhibition, with other less well-known but equally talented artists. Edmonde Charles-Roux came to know these names as news came through to the war zone, and the protagonists of the project remained in her memory as synonymous with peace regained.

When Edmonde Charles-Roux returned to civilian life, her work for Elle, Vogue, les Lettres Françaises, and other magazines brought her once again into the realm of fashion and theater.

It is natural that she should evoke here these friends, some of whom have disappeared, who gave substance with such talent to a project which then represented hope and which was called the Théâtre de la Mode.

The Decorators

André Beaurepaire

Born in Paris in 1924

Scion of a well-to-do paper manufacturing dynasty, as a child André Beaurepaire built imaginary cities on paper. Fantastical perspectives and baroque columns are interwoven in his drawings. Still very young when he exhibited for the first time, he was discovered by the Paris art world and stage directors, thanks to the Théâtre de la Mode. The youngest of the artists involved, Beaurepaire was only twenty years old, with large ears, full lips, black curls that fell over his forehead, and curious sideburns that made him look like a Spanish dancer.

After an exhibition under the aegis of Jean Cocteau in 1947, he signed his first contract with the Wildenstein Gallery in New York, a contract that was renewed regularly until the death of George Wildenstein in 1963.

Beaurepaire's vistas of imaginary cities reaching for the clouds, his buildings tottering as if struck by some Wagnerian Götterdammerung, were subsequently shown in 1965 at The Iolas Gallery in Geneva, and in 1977 by Henriette Gomes in Paris.

Beaurepaire has also had a brilliant career as a set designer. At the suggestion of Christian Bérard, Cocteau commissioned him in 1946 to design the sets for *L'Aigle à deux têtes*, which met with considerable success. Jean Genet turned to him for *Haute Surveillance*. In 1947 he was solicited by London's Covent Garden to create the sets for *Scènes de ballet* with music by Stravinsky and starring Margot Fonteyn. The year 1953 ushered in a long period of collaboration between André Beaurepaire, the Roland Petit Ballet, and Boris Kochno. Beaurepaire designed the sets for seven ballets, including *Sleeping Beauty* (1955) with Leslie Caron, Léo Ferré's *La Nuit* in 1958 with Zizi Jeanmaire, and in 1978 *The Queen of Spades* with Mikhaïl Barychnikov. He has also

designed opera sets, in particular Prokofiev's *la Cenerentola* at La Scala in Milan in 1956, and Gian Carlo Menotti's *Le Dernier Sauvage*. André Beaurepaire is that artist who, in the words of Jean Cocteau, represents "the marriage, alas so rare, of poetry and precision."

Christian Bérard

Born and died in Paris (1902-1949)

The only son of an architect, Christian Bérard was a good student at the Lycée Janson-de-Sailly, a school to which the Paris 16th-arrondissement bourgeoisie have always sent their offspring and, for that matter, still do. From this crucible for sons of well-to-do families with brilliant futures emerged a dreamy, chubby, shy young man with but one desire: to paint.

At eighteen, Christian Bérard entered the Académie Ranson, where he had Maurice Denis and Edouard Vuillard as teachers, and as friends, two Russian students, brothers, natives of St. Petersburg and painters both, Leonide and Eugène Berman. That was the beginning of his lifelong career as an unusual artist forever torn between his love of painting and his love for the theater. Bérard, known as "Bébé," was the most celebrated and bohemian of the sons of the Parisian bourgeoisie, a great-hearted charmer dressed like a bum, a dirty, bearded, long-haired magician who was the darling of theatrical circles and French high society.

His first Paris exhibition, at twenty-three, took place within the framework of a not insignificant although short-lived, ultra-cosmopolitan movement known as the Neo-Humanists, which included the brothers Berman, Tchelitchev, and another Russian by the name of Hosiasson who was born in Odessa. They all advocated a return to Latin classicism.

At twenty-seven Bérard was on the verge of entering "history" in the entourage of Serge de Diaghilev, who commissioned him to design the sets for *Coppelia*. Diaghilev, the most famous and daring spirit in the history of modern ballet, died in Venice in 1929, which put an end to the project.

However, Bérard had made, in the person of Diaghilev's close collaborator Boris Kochno, a determining encounter. It was Kochno who started Bérard on his career in the theater with *Cotillon* for the Ballets Russes de Monte-Carlo (music by Chabrier, choreography by Balanchine), where he soon made a name for himself with his novel ideas and amazingly simple means. The year was 1932. Bérard designs for *Cotillon* foreshadowed those he was to design thirteen years later for the Théâtre de la Mode. *Cotillon* was an instant success. Bérard's set consisted of a theater surrounded by several superimposed rows of spectators' boxes lined with red velvet. The various tableaux had such titles as "Présentation" and "Danse des Chapeaux." Under Boris Kochno's delicate lighting, dancers in long star-studded tutus presented their version of Paris haute couture's latest creations. When in 1945 Robert Ricci gave Bérard overall responsibility for the Théâtre de la Mode's presentation, he knew he was dealing with a seasoned scenographer. Bérard had ten hectic years behind him of uninterrupted theatrical success. He had worked with famous authors Cocteau and Giraudoux–and universally acclaimed directors such as Jouvet and Barrault. But he had only four years to live, always at the same furious tempo, and with the same amazing drive, until one tragic evening he collapsed and died on stage, struck down like Molière, as he was putting the finishing touch to the set for *Les Fourberies de Scapin* for Jean-Louis Barrault. The heart that, as Colette put it, had "guided all the infatuations of Paris, without the slightest ulterior motive," had given out.

André Beaurepaire

Christian Bérard

179

Eliane Bonabel

Eliane Bonabel

Born and died in Paris (1920-2000)

Orphaned at a very early age. Eliane Bonabel was brought up by her grandmother and one of her uncles, a talented violinist. Young Eliane was gifted for drawing and at thirteen was sent to a school for professional training in the Rue Legendre. Her first commission dates from that time. Céline, who was a friend of the family, asked her to illustrate *Journey to the End of Night*. At eighteen she illustrated a book by Count Gobineau, *Akrivie Phrangopoulo*, and then went on to study under Paul Colin. Baron Guy de Rothschild also chose her for the illustration of the only work of fiction he ever wrote, *Aile d'argent la magique*. But the great adventure of her life began when the creativity of this young designer came to the attention of Robert Ricci, who asked her to invent a small-scale, lightweight mannequin that would be easy to move about, for use in the Théâtre de la Mode. Her design was accepted and given to Jean Saint-Martin to execute, which signalled the beginning of a long and fruitful partnership. Their business continued to turn out mannequins until 1968. Meanwhile, Eliane Bonabel also continued to draw. Such leading couturiers as Rochas and Jacques Fath gave her commissions; she did window displays for Hermès, went on tours to lecture on the art of table setting, and continued to illustrate the works of Céline.

Jean Cocteau

Born and died near Paris (Maisons-Laffitte 1889 – Milly-la-Forêt 1963)

Jean Cocteau grew up in a well-to-do bourgeois milieu. This poet, artist, novelist, librettist, and filmmaker who was to become the most Parisian of men of letters, responsible for the discovery of any number

Jean Cocteau

180

of major talents, failed his high school exams, and for the rest of his life had the worst possible memories of his years at the Lycée Condorcet. Like Bérard and many other of his contemporaries, Jean Cocteau owed his début to Serge de Diaghilev and the Ballets Russes, for whom he created two ballets, both initially failures: the first, in 1912, *The Blue God*, with Nijinski, and then *Parade*, which created a huge scandal when it opened in 1917 but remains one of the most significant ballets of its time.

When those in charge of the Théâtre de la Mode invited Jean Cocteau in 1945 to contribute to their hazardous project, he had been steeped in filmmaking, an art he called the "tenth Muse." Cocteau had already written and directed a film called *Blood of a Poet*, a work that in 1930 had drawn attention to a new avant-garde and instantly provoked the wrath of the Surrealists. It had also made clear that Cocteau was unusually gifted in the domain of scenic effects. From 1940 to 1943 Cocteau had also written film dialogues and the script for *L'Eternel Retour*, which came out during the Occupation.

For Cocteau, the Théâtre de la Mode was an opportunity to pay tribute to René Clair, the man responsible for such films as *Paris qui dort*, *Sous les toits de Paris*, *A nous la liberté* and *Quatorze-Juillet*. He wished to honor the most characteristically French filmmaker, the author of films that had most subtly depicted the very essence of Paris.

His tribute to René Clair was a variation on his dreamlike themes. The scene he imagined was a dream — almost a hallucination. Held in contempt by the Surrealists, Cocteau had put their ideas to good use. The set he designed for the Théâtre de la Mode proved that, fifteen years after *Blood of a Poet*, he had lost none of his mastery.

AndréDignimont

André Dignimont

Born and died in Paris (1891-1965)

A life history full of gaps. We shall never know, for instance, why this happy-go-lucky fellow, whom Colette dubbed "le grand Dig," and who first went to a school run by the Oratorian fathers in France, then went to Beckenham College in Brighton, England, where he became captain of the cricket team. He worked in the city for a while, but soon lost his job. Young Dignimont came back to France, where he liked to sport checkered trousers, tweed caps, and short pipes *à l'anglaise*: a form of elegance also affected by Braque and Derain. The year was 1910. Dignimont's studio contained an unbelievable collection of bric-à-brac. There were pipes, opalines, hat forms, and a hurdy-gurdy, while antique chamberpots on the floor held old parasols. Dignimont lived on the Ile Saint-Louis. As Roland Dorgelès wrote: "He had the Seine for a confidant and the morgue for a neighbor."

None of the artists of the Théâtre de la Mode was as devoted to literary circles as Dignimont. Colette was his friend, Mac Orlan and Francis Carco were his sidekicks. Like them, he hung around in shady bars and public dance halls and frequented the lower depths of Paris as depicted by Toulouse-Lautrec: that of disreputable characters and brothels.

André Dignimont specialized in two things. He designed theater sets and, at the time of the Théâtre de la Mode, he had just completed the sets for the Paris Opera production of *Guignol et Pandore*, a ballet by Serge Lifar and avant-garde composer André Jolivet. He was also an illustrator who throughout his life enriched the French publishing scene with his works and many beautiful books, among them works by Balzac, Zola, Oscar Wilde, Alain-Fournier, Huysmans, and his lifelong friend Colette.

Georges Douking

Born and died in Paris (1902-1987)

He wore thick bangs in the manner of Foujita. His name was not Douking but Ladoubée. Why this *nom de guerre*, and why Douking? No one knows. He had piercing eyes, a tormented face, and a strong personality.

Douking had had a difficult start in life. Born of a humble family in which everyone could draw, he fell so ill at the age of fifteen that he had to give up his studies at the Ecole des Arts et Métiers. While doing his military service he studied music, and as soon as he returned to civilian life he became a *chansonnier*. He sang at the Théâtre des Deux-Anes and the Cabaret de Dix-Heures, after which he studied dance while also continuing to study painting, which he had begun in 1918.

Georges Douking

The director and famous theatrical theorist Gaston Baty was to Douking what Charles Dullin was to Touchagues. He gave him a role in *Crime and Punishment* at the Théâtre Montparnasse, commissioned him to design a set and employed him as stage manager for four years. In 1937, Douking made his debut as a freelance stage manager at the Théâtre des Ambassadeurs, where he indulged his taste for such foreign playwrights as Synge, Kleist, and Bruchner.

When Douking was asked to contribute to the Théâtre de la Mode, he had just made headlines at the Théâtre Hébertot as director of *Sodom and Gomorrah*, a play by Giraudoux with sets and costumes by Bérard, lighting by Boris Kochno, and music by Honegger. Fame was just around the corner, and Douking went on to become the tireless servant of contemporary theater with his sets for plays by Marcel Aymé, Armand Salacrou, and Vercors.

Georges Geffroy

Georges Geffroy

Born and died in Paris (1905-1971)

Born of a well-to-do Protestant family, he was brought up by his mother, surrounded by the rare and valuable objects collected by his father, who was killed in 1917 during World War I. Georges Geffroy from a very early age was a knowledgeable collector himself. He had a passion for buying Eighteenth-century furniture, and was so well known as a connoisseur of antiques that wealthy Parisians set great store by his advice.

He started out making fashion drawings and even worked as a stylist for Patou. Soon, however, he was working fulltime as an interior decorator. He was a close friend of Christian Dior, whom he had met in the 1930s, and with whom he shared a well-defined and classical taste devoid of any anglomania. Apartments decorated by Geffroy had in common superb furniture, the use of off-white and beige, few bright colors but many pale solids, often fabric-covered walls, many door curtains, all slightly conventional and somewhat formal. With Victor Grandpierre he decorated part of Christian Dior's townhouse, when the latter, once an obscure art dealer, had become rich and famous as a couturier and moved to the Boulevard Jules-Sandeau.

At the time that Georges Geffroy worked for the Théâtre de la Mode and on the show's interior decoration for its tour of the United States, his reputation was that of a man with a brilliant future, a demanding decorator with rigorous standards who worked with the very best of French craftsmen.

Emili Grau-Sala

Born in Barcelona, died in Paris (1911-1975)

Like his senior, Joan Rebull, Grau-Sala was a Catalan. Taught by the Fathers of Saint-Joseph, he only finished grade school and then went on to study painting at the School of Fine Arts in Barcelona, a veritable nursery for artists, where Picasso's father had taught drawing. There Grau-Sala met a student of his own age, a young house painter named Antoni Clavé, who was very poor and could only attend evening classes. They remained friends in Paris as well, and like Rebull and Clavé, Grau-Sala followed Picasso's example and settled in Paris in the 1930s, as had Manolo, Gargallo, Fenoso, and many others. Catalans were everywhere in Paris and easy to spot. They all knew Picasso, and some were influenced by him.

Emili Grau-Sala

Boris Kochno

This was not the case of Emili Grau-Sala who, upon his arrival in Paris, came under the spell of Vuillard's soft colors and tender domestic scenes, a genre that determined his career. An artist who recorded scenes from everyday life, as he did in the tableau he created for the Théâtre de la Mode, Grau-Sala was also known as a brilliant illustrator with a light, subtle, and occasionally perverse touch, as well as a theatrical designer. Among his illustrations to be remembered are his watercolors for the four volumes of Colette's *Claudine* and his work in dry point for *Gigi* and *Chéri*.

Boris Kochno

Born in Moscow, died in Paris (1904-1990)

He went to school in Moscow and was only sixteen when his mother left Russia at the height of the Revolution and took him to France. Boris Kochno was a very dark, very slim, very handsome young man who wrote poetry. As soon as he had settled in Paris, he cast about for support in the only circles he knew, those of Russian émigrés. A painter twenty years his senior, member of the Moscow school, Sergei Yourievitch Soudeïkine, who had also left Russia forever, offered to introduce Kochno to Serge de Diaghilev. He knew the latter well and had been commissioned by him in 1912 to create his first sets for *La Tragédie de Salomé*, with the great Karsavina, on whose knee he would paint a rose before every performance.

Serge de Diaghilev was looking for a secretary. He received Boris Kochno at the Hotel Scribe on February 27, 1921, and hired him.

Boris Kochno joined the Ballets Russes at a time of transition. Nijinski was no longer king and the fairylike Karsavina had opted for England. New stars were appearing on the horizon: a dancer from Kiev named Serge Lifar and Balanchine. Kochno became Diaghilev's artistic adviser and, during the final period of the Ballets Russes, it was he who pressed for a change in direction. He stepped up the pace of modernization, especially in the choice of musicians. He produced librettos for ballets including *Les Fâcheux* (1924), *Les Matelots* (1925), *La Chatte* (1927), *Ode* (1928) and *The Prodigal Son* (1929) – the masterworks of his Diaghilev days.

Between 1929, the time of Diaghilev's death in Venice, and his contribution to the success of the

Théâtre de la Mode in 1944, Boris Kochno had acquired a unique reputation as the greatest living authority on ballet. His lighting had wrought marvels on many a French and foreign stage. His advice and collaboration were solicited in every conceivable domain. The name of Boris Kochno on a program was proof of originality and perfectionism. For a long time following World War II, nothing could be undertaken without him. His legendary good taste, his incurable Slavic accent and thunderously rolling Rs, his extraordinary handwriting with its consummately artful arabesques all were – and still are – part and parcel of his legend. The book he wrote, entitled *Diaghilev and the Ballets Russes*, records the extent of his unique knowledge.

Jean-Denis Malclès

Born and died in Paris (1912-2002)

Jean-Denis Malclès was born of a sculptor father and a painter mother, originally from Avignon. His family had always had a taste for literature. One of his great-uncles was the poet Joseph Roumanille, who wrote in Provencal, founded the "Félibrige" with Frédéric Mistral, and became its publisher. His parents expected him to devote himself to the decorative arts, but Jean-Denis Malclès preferred stage sets, painting, and illustration. He studied at the prestigious Ecole Boulle, which provided training in interior decoration and woodwork techniques. His first employer was the most famous decorator of the 1930s, Ruhlmann, who specialized in formal furniture, decorating important embassies, great floating cities such as the ocean-liner the Ile-de-France, and famous restaurants (Drouant); and who was commissioned by leading fashion designers (Caroline Reboux and Madame Paquin), well-known bankers (Worms and Rothschild), and such prominent figures as the Maharajah of Indore, the Viceroy of India, and Lord Rothermere. Ruhlmann, whose designs have now become collectors' items, always selected his draftsmen from the students of the Ecole Boulle. His choice fell on Malclès, whose apprenticeship was no bed of roses. Before long, however, Malclès had to make a choice. He decided not to become another craftsman specializing in lacquerwork, shark-skin and ivory-studded ebony, and gave up the world of furniture. He turned to painting, devoting his gift for invention to a typically Parisian "salon" which at that time was one of great prestige, the Salon de l'Imagerie. There he was in charge of coordinating the work of artists who designed upholstery fabrics, posters, and wallpaper. Malclès' talent drew the attention of Christian Bérard, who asked him to contribute to the Théâtre de la Mode. By then Malclès was no newcomer to set

Jean-Denis Malclès

design. In 1941, Pierre Bertin had given him a theatrical commission and Malclès had been hailed as the discovery of the year. His sets for *Fantasio*, a Comédie-Française production, had been a sensational hit.

Malclès was a master of magical effects, and gave his all to the set he designed for the Théâtre de la Mode. He later surpassed his own reputation with the costumes he created for the Frères Jacques and his sets for Jean Anouilh's major plays. His name became synonymous, in fact, with that of the author of *Ardèle ou la Marguerite* and *La Valse des toréadors*, so much so that to recount the career of stage designer Jean-Denis Malclès is to describe part of French theatrical history in the aftermath of World War II.

Joan Rebull

Born in Reus, died in Barcelona (1899-1981)

Little is know about this Catalan who lived in Paris, whom the Bénézit *Dictionary of Painters, Sculptors, Illustrators and Engravers* describes in the briefest of terms: "Rebull, sculptor born in Catalonia, active in the Twentieth century (Spanish school)." It is very little for an artist whom Picasso honored with his friendship. Fortunately, the journalist Louis Cheronnet, former editor-in-chief of the magazine *Art et Décoration*, and the true historian of

Théâtre de la Mode tells us more about him. If it were not for him, how would we have known that Rebull was born in Reus in Catalonia? It was there he first saw the light of day at the very end of the Nineteenth century. At the age of ten he was carving wood in a workshop that produced religious statues. He was so skillful that his native town awarded him a scholarship, and at the age of sixteen he went off to study at the School of Fine Arts in Barcelona, while continuing to earn a living as a craftsman in a workshop.

A Barcelona banker who recognized the boy's unusual talent helped him financially, which made it possible for Rebull to devote himself entirely to the art of sculpture. He was twenty-two when he received a scholarship to study abroad, first in London, then in Paris. The French capital made such an impression on young Rebull that he remained there from 1926 to 1930. The following year was a turning point, for in 1931 the Spanish Republic was proclaimed and Rebull was elected to the Parliament of Catalonia. In 1934 he was in Tarragona, in charge of the School of Fine Arts of the State of Catalonia.

In 1938 the Republican government sent Rebull to Paris to execute sculptures for the Spanish Pavilion at the New York World's Fair. With the victory of Franco's troops, he chose not to return to Spain, but to remain in exile in Paris where he installed himself in a Left Bank studio under the eaves of an old house. Among his books, there was one he cherished above all others, one that bore a dedication by Picasso dated June 1944. His Catalan friend Picasso had drawn on the book's cover a bearded man's head wearing a "barretina" or beret worn by Catalan fishermen.

It was in this studio, wrapped in his coat with a woolen scarf around his neck – the winter was icy and there was no heating – that Joan Rebull received Ricci's commission for the heads of the mannequins for the Théâtre de la Mode, which he sculpted with such rare delicacy.

Joan Rebull

Jean Saint-Martin

Jean Saint-Martin

Born and died in Paris (1899-1988)

Born of a lower middle-class family, Jean Saint-Martin was interested in sculpture. Business was bad, however, in his father's braid and trimmings factory, and he was unable to go to the school of his choice. At the age of sixteen, he was apprenticed to a manufacturer of wax mannequins, the house of Siegel, where he was able to deploy his talent as a sculptor on the heads of the mannequins. This experience, which lasted ten years, in 1920 launched him on a fascinating adventure at the side of an exceptional man who lived his era to the fullest, André Vigneau (1892-1968). The house of Siegel had commissioned him to design mannequins of an entirely new kind for the Decorative Arts Exhibition of 1925, and they had been an enormous success. When, a few years later, Vigneau decided to devote himself to photography and opened the first major advertising studio in Paris, Jean Saint-Martin left Siegel and went into partnership with him. Photographer André Vigneau knew how to pick his collaborators. In 1931, he acquired a first-rate assistant by the name of Robert Doisneau.

While engaging in other activities, Jean Saint-Martin continued to create mannequins with Eliane Bonabel. His technique was most original, for Jean Saint-Martin's mannequins were made of zinc-plated wiring. The painter and well-known publicist, Cassandre, was the first to notice and to use them. It was also Cassandre who encouraged Saint-Martin to specialize in the decoration of interiors and fashion boutiques, a field in which he was to excel.

In 1944, Jean Saint-Martin was commissioned by Robert Ricci to execute the prototype for the miniature mannequin designed by Eliane Bonabel for the Théâtre de la Mode, and he interpreted that design in his own technique.

The partnership between Saint-Martin and Eliane Bonabel that began in 1945 lasted for a long and fruitful time. They created a joint business of their own, which remained in operation till 1968.

Emilio Terry

Born in Cuba, died in Paris (1890-1969)

The son of wealthy Spanish planters in Cuba, Emilio Terry was a self-taught artist who was free to choose his own teachers and to study as he wanted, far from any school or academy, concentrating on the study of old treatises and rare books, for he could afford to buy them. All he cared about was architecture and drawing well, and his only mentors were Palladio and Ledoux. Like a pianist practicing his scales for years on end, Terry did nothing but fill notebook after notebook – 400 of them – with his designs. He devised rockwork consoles, pavilions, enchanted grottos, and furniture that sprouted roots.

An independent loner, rich enough and with sufficient connections in French high society, Terry was neither a dandy nor a worldly *bon vivant*. He spent his life doing exactly as he pleased. He was free to choose his clients and to accept only those commissions that appealed to him, and he used his freedom to the hilt.

The first hint of recognition came in 1922, when a Swiss banker commissioned him to design a small beach house in Lutry on the banks of Lake Leman. It was as graceful as a miniature Palladian villa. That was

only the beginning. Emilio Terry was over forty when he started to make a name for himself in 1933, the year he first showed his drawings and maquettes at the Galerie Bonjean, where some of his friends named Dali, Jean Hugo, Christian Bérard, Eugène Berman, and Tchelitchev also showed their work. Parts of Terry's Paris show were shown at the Museum of Modern Art in New York a few years later. Well before that, however, he had been recognized in Paris as an architect, and his career had taken off. In 1933, he designed sets for Balanchine's ballets and furniture for Jean-Michel Frank. These two commissions heralded his 1938 encounter with two arbiters of French taste, Charles, Vicomte de Noailles–who commissioned grotto-specialist Terry to design an alcove-terrace for his house in Grasse–and the fabulously wealthy Mexican, Charles de Bestegui, owner of the Château de Groussay, for whom he executed every conceivable whim and fancy: follies all over the grounds, pavilions, enchanted bridges, pyramids, a private theater, and décors for balls. Emilio Terry managed to revitalize the baroque and to present late Eighteenth-century designs in a new light; a critic described his refurbished and purified neoclassicism as nothing less than a whole new style, which he called "Louis XVII." Small wonder that Emilio Terry's set for the Théâtre de la Mode was a pure example of his art. Eliane Bonabel's mannequins, clothed in creations by Jean Dessès, Grès, and Worth, were silhouetted against a background of an enchanted grotto, stonework, rocks, and pavilions worthy of Ledoux, the favorite shapes and key components in the artistic vocabulary of Emilio Terry, the most Parisian of Cubans.

Louis Touchagues

Born at Saint-Cyr-au-Mont-d'Or, died in Paris (1893-1974)

Of Catalan origin, Touchagues was thirty when he left the French provinces for Paris with nothing more than a modest travel grant to his name, but with a determination to make good. He had had little training. He had studied at the School of Fine Arts in Lyon. In Paris he took courses in architecture at the Regnault workshop of the School of Fine Arts, holding down several jobs to survive: as an architect's clerk, fabric designer for Paul Poiret, and assistant stage manager at the Théâtre de l'Atelier, where a man of genius, Charles Dullin, reigned supreme. The latter drove him hard for very little pay. In 1923, Dullin commissioned Touchagues to design his first stage set, for *Monsieur Pygmalion*, written by a Spanish playwright. Those were Touchagues' most heroic, leanest years. It was not long, however, before he had more commissions than he could handle. From 1923 till the time of his death, the name of Touchagues was associated with those of the best writers of light comedy (Achard, Labiche) and that of Charles Dullin, whose official decorator he became.

Touchagues was part of the group that called itself "the Cartel" and which associated Charles Dullin, Louis Jouvet, and Baty, from 1922 till World War II, when new talents by the name of Jean Vilar and Barrault came on the scene. Touchagues identified, in other words, with the halcyon days of prewar theater when decorators did not always have to have genius or imagination, but did have to be professional down to their very fingertips. Touchagues indeed lacked originality but was very much a professional. He also illustrated art books and was highly regarded by members of the Académie Goncourt. Colette, whose *Paris de ma fenêtre* he illustrated, André Salmon, André Billy, and Léon-Paul Fargue, for whom he illustrated *Charme de*

Louis Touchagues

Paris, all had a soft spot in their hearts for Touchagues, a nightowl who loved beautiful girls, painted the world of fashion and did portraits of *Le Tout-Paris* in the 1930s.

He lived in an attic of sorts, decorated in deliberately bad taste, a kind of market stall with windows overlooking the Rue de la Paix. Touchagues did not claim to be the Constantin Guys or Gavarin of his day, although he might occasionally imply that he was. With his dark skin and the looks of a shady character just sprung from jail, he was not without charm or at a loss for words when he would tell the story of Paul Poiret, his first patron, who bought one of his drawings for 400 francs, a sum that in his leaner days seemed an absolute fortune. When Touchagues, the provincial boy who had made good in Paris, worked for the Théâtre de la Mode, he produced a replica of what he saw from his attic window, the Rue de la Paix and the Place Vendôme.

Georges Wakhevitch

Born in Odessa, died in Paris (1907-1984)

Russians from Provence are a very special breed, and Georges Wakhevitch, an émigré and son of an engineer, was one of them. Every Russian who ever arrived from Odessa aboard an old Paquet Steamship Co. cargo that dropped anchor in the harbor of Marseilles, was dazzled by the luminous Provençal sky. Georges Wakhevitch, whose name was to figure on Parisian theater posters for half a century, arrived in France with his mother at the age of fourteen. He did not speak a word of French, and was never to lose the accent that was a blend of Slav and Provençal speech and added to his appeal. "Wakhé," as he was known in theatrical circles, was full of charm. The two years he spent as a high school student in Manosque in Haute-Provence had not rid him of his habit of playing hooky, nor did his three years at the Lycée Buffon in Paris cure him of his passion for painting. At the age of sixteen, he took drawing lessons at La Grande Chaumière. Unable to pay for his studies, he looked around for odd jobs. In the 1930s, Russians were in the forefront of the world of French cinema; producers, cameramen, decorators, and actors were all Russian émigrés, and they all welcomed young Wakhevitch, who hoped to become a decorator. He worked as an extra in the old studios in Montreuil. His first role was that of a bellboy. His failure to pass his baccalauréat exams did the rest, for he knew what he wanted to be: a decorator. He had a hard time making ends meet doing odd jobs. Not caring whether he worked in films or in the theater, he kept an open mind, pursuing his career in both mediums. He received a commission for a first set in Paris, from Lugné-Poë at the Théâtre de l'Œuvre in 1927, then had a great success in Marseilles with André Roussin's Rideau Gris

Georges Wakhevitch

Company in 1930 and finally went on to create his first film set in 1931 at the Victorine studios in Nice.

He was off to a brilliant start as a great set designer. Throughout his busy career he worked on 200 operas, 300 plays and a 140 films. Jean Cocteau, with whom he had created the sets for *L'Eternel Retour* in 1943, introduced Wakhevitch to Robert Ricci, and he was commissioned to create two tableaux for the Théâtre de la Mode.

Wakhevitch was a painter first and last. His maquettes were as finished as a painting. Of all the decorators who worked for the Théâtre de la Mode, he was the only one to imagine a harbor scene, in which a quay and the superimposed arches of an ancient aqueduct were outlined against the sky and afforded a glimpse of the torn sails of a great ship arriving from afar. It was a set depicting all the nostalgia for the quays and ports of call known to every émigré. In his heart of hearts, Wakhevitch remained a Slav.

Biographies translated from the French by Nina de Voogd

The first English edition of this book was created in conjunction with an exhibition organized and held in The Costume Institute of The Metropolitan Museum of Art, New York, from December 8, 1990, through April 14, 1991, in collaboration with the Maryhill Museum of Art, Goldendale, Washington, and the Musée des Arts de la Mode, Paris.

Director of The Metropolitan Museum of Art, Philippe de Montebello.

This exhibition was been made possible by Wolfgang K. Flöttl.

Exhibition Credits

Conceived and organized by Katell le Bourhis

Assistants to Katell le Bourhis:
Natalie Coe
Margaret van Buskirk

Conservation:
Chris Paulocik
Debby Juchem

Mannequin preparation:
June Bove
Joell Kunath

Exhibition decorator:
Richard Giglio

Installation designer and graphics:
David Harvey

Lighting designer:
Zack Zanolli
Gallery music:
Kenneth Moore

The Costume Institute Library:
Robert C. Kaufmann
Sheila Smith

Editorial:
Barbara Burn
Teresa Egan
Pamela K. Barr

The staff of The Costume Institute

Other museum departments, including:
The Office of the Director
Operations
Design
Development
Registrar
Paper Conservation
Prints and Photographs
Public Information
Photograph and Slide Library
Archives
Photograph Studio
and the Information Desk of the Metropolitan Museum of Art

Lender of the Dolls of the Théâtre de la Mode

Maryhill Museum of Art, Goldendale, Washington

Lenders to the Exhibition

Musée des Arts de la Mode
Musée de la Mode et du Costume, Palais Galliera
Balenciaga
Eliane Bonabel
La Chambre Syndicale de la Couture Parisienne
Chaumet
Editions du May
Margaret Floyd
Nadine Gasc
Jean-Denis Malclès
Sylvia Spitzer

Volunteers

Research:
Kirk Allan Adair
Geneviève Dard
Andrea Markinson
Jane Ziegelman

Volunteers for the exhibition:
Kirk Allan Adair
Marianna de Chaunac
Edith de Montebello
Geneviève Dard
Rochelle Friedman
Marilyn Lawrence
Rosalie Lemontree
Brigid Merriman
Bonnie Rosenblum

All docents of The Costume Institute

Special Acknowledgments

André Beaurepaire
Eliane Bonabel
Stanley Garfinkel
Jean-Denis Malclès
Linda Brady Mountain
Pierre Provoyeur
Anne Surgers
Susan Train

Acknowledgements

Benoît d'Aboville; Beth Alberty; Alexandre de Paris; Thomas J. Ball; Véronique Belloir; Pierre Bergé; Jean Bergeron; Jean-Pierre Bertin-Maghit; René Boivin; Boucheron; Bouteron; Eugène Clarence Braun-Munk; Cartier; Chaumet; Annie Cohen-Solal; DEFI - Le Comité de Développement et de Promotion du Textile et de l'Habillement; Robert Currie; Martha Deese; the late Stephen de Pietri; Lillian A. Dickler; Deirdre Donohue; Jean L. Druesedow; Erin Durkin; The Fashion Foundation, Tokyo; La Fédération française de la Couture, du Prêt-à-Porter des couturiers et des Créateurs de la Mode; Kimberly Fink; Wolfgang K. Flöttl; Phylis Fogelson; Nadine Gasc; Caroline Goldthorpe; Goossens; Jacques Grange; François Halard; Marla Hambourg; Joy Henderiks; Catherine Join-Dieterle; Martine Jouhair; Marie-Andrée Jouve; Andrey Kostiw; Pierre Lambertin; Margaret Lawson; Mme J.C. le Bourhis; François Lesage; Betty J. Long; Michèle Majer; Massaro; Lori Meade; Herbert Moskowitz; Jacques Mouclier; Denise Organos; André Ostier; Dominique Pallut; Paulin Paris; Pierre Passebon; Marie-Paule Pellé; Tony Penrose; Béatrice de Plinval; Prigent; Emily Rafferty; Carol Rathore; Antoine Riboud; Pierre de Rohan Chabot; Jeff Rosenheim; John Ross; Suzy Rubin; Jean-Jacques de Saint Andrieu; Yves Saint Laurent; Roger Schall; Jean Seeberger; David Seidner; Cindy Sirko; Linda Sylling; Dominick Tallarico; Mahrukh Tarapor; Alecander Thomson; Van Cleef & Arpels; Marla Weinhoff.

Maryhill Museum of Art

Maryhill Museum of Art is located high above the Columbia River in the Pacific Northwest, near Goldendale, Washington. A private mansion built at the beginning of the century, and dedicated in 1926 by Queen Marie of Roumania, it opened to the public as a museum of art in 1940. Important collections were donated by Queen Marie of Roumania, Loïe Fuller, and Alma de Bretteville Spreckels, friends of the founder Samuel Hill. Those collections include European and American paintings, Russian icons, antique furniture, French decorative art glass by Gallé and Lalique, as well as a remarkable collection of Auguste Rodin sculptures. Since it opened, the museum has developed ethnographic collections of the nation's native peoples and a large collection of international chess sets. The museum has grown and developed over the years, now regularly exhibiting contemporary Northwest art and sculpture. The mannequins of the Théâtre de la Mode were donated to Maryhill Museum by the Chambre Syndicale de la Couture in 1952 and are now part of the museum's permanent collections.

The museum would like to thank the following Maryhill volunteers for their assistance with the Théâtre de la Mode over the past 14 years of its reemergence. Without you and many others it would have been impossible.

Bonnie Beeks, Helen Juris, Deborah Gotts, Donette Love, Jeanney McArthur, Phyllis McDermid, Denise Morris, Pam Rapach, Helen Thomson, Jean Thompson, Beverly Wheelhouse, Juanita Carpenter, Kathleen McKinney, Wendy Hodges, Dan Ellis, Robin Hudson, Fred Henchell, Jeanne Marks, Beverly Zaremba, Ron Zaremba, Kathy Mitchell, Schommer & Sons, Friberg Electric.

Maryhill Museum of Art

35 Maryhill Museum Drive
Goldendale, WA, 98620
Telephone: (509)773-3733
E-mail: maryhill@maryhillmuseum.org

For information on the Théâtre de la Mode video, go to www.maryhillmuseum.org

Maryhill Museum of Art Staff - 2002

Colleen Schafroth, Executive Director
Patricia Perry, Operations Manager
Betty Long-Schleif, Collections Manager
Lee Musgrave, Public Relations Officer
Celia Killeen, Development Officer
Courtney Spousta, Curator of Education
Christine Lewallen, Administrative
  Secretary
Carolyn Clark, Museum Assistant

Maryhill Museum of Art Staff – 1990

Linda Brady Mountain, Director
Colleen Schafroth, Curator of Education
Betty Long, Registrar
Ross Randall, Public Relations Officer
Patricia Perry, Operations Manager
Cheryl Cameron, Museum staff
George Bringman, Museum staff

An article in the July 30, 1952, Oregon Journal

Théâtre de la Mode Time Line with page references

Index

Photo Credits

David Seidner photos ©1990 International Center of Photography, David Seidner Archive

front cover: Laurent Sully-Jaulmes
Page 1:   David Seidner
Page 2:   Bonabel Archives
Page 5:   Laurent Sully-Jaulmes
Page 10:   David Seidner
Page 11:   Condé Nast publications
Page 13:   Christian Berard
Pages 14-15: Pierre Jahan
Page17:   Laurent Sully-Jaulmes
Page 19:   Bonabel Archives
Page 21:   Robert Doisneau/Rapho
Page 22:   Andre Ostier
Page 23:   Ronny Jaques
Pages 24-25: Robert Doisneau/Rapho
Pages 26-30: Lee Miller Archives
Page 31:   Lee Miller Archives/courtesy of Condé Nast Publications
Pages 32-35: Lee Miller Archives
Page 36:   Robert Doisneau/Rapho
Page 37:   Lee Miller Archives
Pages 38-39: Seeberger/Bibliotheque Nationale, Paris
Page 40:   Robert Doisneau/Rapho
Page 41:   Ronny Jaques
Page 43:   top: André Ostier,
             bottom left: Pierre Boucher
             bottom right: Robert Doisneau/Rapho
Page 45:   André Ostier
Page 47:   top left: Seeberger/Bibliotheque Nationale, Paris; bottom left: Robert Doisneau/Rapho, right: Bonabel Archives
Page 48:   top: Ronny Jaques, bottom: André Ostier
Page 49:   Bonabel Archives (Berard drawing/SPADEM)
Page 50:   top: Roger Schall bottom: Laurent Sully-Jaulmes
Page 51:   Laurent Sully-Jaulmes
Pages 52-53: top left: R.R., top right: Roger Schall bottom: Laurent Sully-Jaulmes
Pages 54-55: top right: Roger Schall bottom: Laurent Sully-Jaulmes
Pages 56-57: top left: Roger Schall bottom: Laurent Sully-Jaulmes
Pages 58-59: bottom left: R.R.; bottom right: Roger Schall top: Laurent Sully-Jaulmes
Page 60:   top: Laurent Sully-Jaulmes bottom: Roger Schall

Page 61:   Laurent Sully-Jaulmes
Page 62:   top: Laurent Sully-Jaulmes bottom: Roger Schall
Page 63:   top: Laurent Sully-Jaulmes bottom: Roger Schall bottom right: R.R.
Pages 64-65: top left: R.R., Roger Schall,
Page 66:   Bonabel Archives
Page 68:   Philip Roedel
Page 69:   Ronny Jaques
Page 71:   photographer unknown
Page 72:   Ronny Jaques
Page 73:   Horst/Courtesy Vogue 1946-1974 by Condé Nast Publications Inc.
Page 74:   Ronny Jaques
Page 76:   Lee Miller Archives
Page 78:   Seeberger Bibliotheque Nationale, Paris
Page 79:   Lee Miller Archives
Page 80:   Francois Kollar/Ministere de la Culture
Pages 81-82: Seebergeer Bibliotheque Nationale, Paris
Pages 83-88: Laurent Sully-Jaulmes
Page 89:   Ronny Jaques
Page 91:   Laurent Sully-Jaulmes
Pages 92-93: Rene Gruau
Pages 94-95: Willy Maywald/Archives Dior ©2002 Artists Rights Society (ARS), New York/ADAGP, Paris
Pages 97-128: David Seidner
Pages 129-166: Laurent Sully-Jaulmes
Page 167:   top: Maryhill Museum of Art archives: bottom: Laurent Sully-Jaulmes
Pages 168-172: Maryhill Museum of Art Archives
Page 173:   top: Pati Palmer, bottom: Maryhill Museum of Art Archives
Pages 174-175: Pati Palmer
Page 176:   top: Maryhill Museum of Art Archives; bottom: Storm Photo. Kingston, N.Y.
Page 178:   Lee Miller Archives
Page 179:   top: André Ostier, bottom: Lee Miller Archives
Page 180:   top: Bonabel Archives, bottom: Lee Miller Archives
Page 181:   top: Bonabel Archives, bottom: R.R.
Page 182:   Andre Ostier
Page 183:   left: R.R., right: André Ostier
Page 184:   R.R.
Page 185:   top: Robert Doisneau/Rapho bottom: Andre Ostier
Page 186:   Archives Francois de la Tour d'Auvergne
Page 187:   Seeberger Bibliotheque Nationale, Paris
Page 189:   top: Rob Reynolds, Reynolds/Wolf Design Inc. bottom: Maryhill Museum of Art Archives
back cover: David Seidner

First Edition Designed by
Richard Medioni and Francoise Bosquet.

Second Edition Designed by
Linda Wisner